OUTRAGEOUS
AND
COURAGEOUS

FRED BERNHARD
and
JEREMY ASHWORTH

WESTBOW°
PRESS
A DIVISION OF THOMAS NELSON
& ZONDERVAN

Special thanks to the following for the cover photo:
Photography – Fiona Grant of Seattle, WA. (www.fionagrantblog.com)
Coordination – Luther's Table of Renton, WA. (www.lutherstable.org)

To view the story of the cover photo and the Study Guide for the book, please visit our website; www.e3ministrygroup.com

WestBow Press books may be ordered through booksellers or by contacting:

WestBow Press
A Division of Thomas Nelson & Zondervan
1663 Liberty Drive
Bloomington, IN 47403
www.westbowpress.com
1 (866) 928-1240

ISBN: 978-1-4908-2278-5 (sc)
ISBN: 978-1-4908-2279-2 (e)

Library of Congress Control Number: 2014900735

Printed in the United States of America.

WestBow Press rev. date: 03/04/2014

CONTENTS

FOREWORD

We never meant to write a book. This isn't false modesty, and we're not kidding.

It started off so innocently. I (Jeremy) was asked "Can you help do a photo shoot for a book cover?" Sure. "Can you help edit just one chapter of a book?" Why not? Pretty soon Fred & Jeremy found themselves neck-deep in the mishmash of soul-searching and word-smithing that is honest-to-God book writing. And there was no turning back.

It's like at church when someone asks you to tell the children's story. "It's easy! It's a short-term commitment! You'd be great!" Pretty soon you wake up and you're leading the whole children's ministry department and hosting teen lock-ins on the weekend. You don't know if you got suckered into saying yes or if the Holy Spirit was at work. Or both.

Of course there came a point where we made a choice: We are doing this. We chose to be carried along not just by circumstances, but by our passion and calling. We are pastors. We love people. We love Jesus. We live and breathe to connect people to people and people to God through Jesus Christ. At its best, the organized church can be the place where the Great Commandment and Great Commission come together. But the undeniable reality is that too many churches are struggling. This combination of problems (in our churches) and passions (for people and for the gospel) keeps us awake at night, and we wanted to do something about it.

This book is full of stories, and you should know that every single tale is true. In some cases we've changed the names or identifying details to protect the innocent (or the guilty!), and some characters are composites, but these real-life events happened to people we know firsthand.

And there are two more stories we need to tell.

The first story takes place in a cozy, wooded Christian camp in southern Ohio. A small group of young teenagers were sitting by a crackling fire when the subject of church came up. One young man belonged to a local congregation that was really growing. He talked about how his pastor was leading the charge for a vital ministry with awesome impact. But in this fireside chat, the pastor's vision wasn't celebrated, and the young man's tone carried a subtle suspicion about the motives of his minister. A different young man around the bonfire, who belonged to a different congregation, quickly became incensed. It only took a spark, but now the fire was burning. "Your pastor must be full of himself! Who does he think he is? What egotism! What selfish ambition!" It didn't take much for him to cast aspersions on a pastor he had never met.

The incensed young man was Jeremy. The pastor was Fred.

So why do I (Jeremy) share this with you now? Aside from the divine irony that my coauthor, unbeknownst to him, was once the target of my seriously misplaced outrage?

I (Jeremy) will say that I have been blessed to have a handful of life-changing and eclectic mentors, men who have poured their lives into mine and have shaped my soul. Almost all of my mentors have been excellent critical thinkers. But this great strength - critical thinking - somehow got twisted after it took root in my heart and mind. Instead of being a critical thinker, more often I would just be critical. And I got to be good at it.

It has taken me too long to realize that the critic's couch is a chronically comfortable and deeply seductively safe place to sit.

We feel powerful and sophisticated, even though nothing really happens. We are protected from failure by virtue of never having made an effort, and hide behind theoretical principles we can never be bothered to actually embody. Too often, criticism is nothing more than animated cowardice. I know because I've been there, an infallible non-participant. And I've had plenty of company.

I share my story with you because it partially answers the question of why we wrote this book. When it comes to both relationships and to evangelism, *criticism is not enough*. That's our four-word foreword.

It's not enough to be an armchair expert on all the ways other people butcher evangelism and screw up relationships. Disparagement isn't a ministry. The Great Commandment and the Great Commission are not fulfilled by pointing out the ways others don't fulfill them. Put yourself out there! Risk failure and make something happen! There is a reason that the Bible describes "mockers" as those who "sit in seats" (Psalm 1:1). Get off the couch. Get in the ring.

This book is our attempt to lead by example, however faltering. We're willing to make a fool of ourselves in front of God and everybody in the effort to help the Great Commandment and Great Commission come alive in our churches. Our salvation comes from the fact that in Jesus, God has skin in the game. So should we. Because that story is true as well.

Blessings,
Fred Bernhard & Jeremy Ashworth

PS – Remember how we said there were two stories we needed to tell? The second story is about the photos on the front and back cover of this book, and you can find out more by going to http://www.e3ministrygroup.com/

Chapter 1

A MORE EXCELLENT WAY

Unholy Terror

Everybody has a bad evangelism story. Here is Fred's.

It promised to be exciting, but the first part of the conference was predictable. Led by a large local church, it was nothing more than a lecture about the pastor's faith-sharing philosophy. The conference also promised to be educational. On this point it delivered, but the lessons seared into my heart that day weren't found in the curriculum.

After the speech, we were divided into small teams, each led by a person from the sponsoring church. We were handed the name and address of one household in the immediate area. The task? Cold-call evangelism. When finished, we'd report back to the others at the conference.

Off we went. We knocked. The door opened. The woman who greeted us was old enough to be my mother. She was not expecting visitors but politely invited us inside. She did not recognize me, but I immediately realized she was a member of a neighboring congregation.

We were barely seated in the living room before our leader cut to the chase. "Are you saved? Do you know that for sure? If you died tomorrow …?" The one-way torrent was not a genuine inquiry but an interrogation with a deadline. His questions were fast-paced and intense. Her responses were slow and timid. But each time, his hard question received her soft answer. Yes. I squirmed and considered her unbelievably gracious for not throwing us out.

Unfortunately, our feckless leader was just getting started. Despite the plain meaning of her answer, he interpreted her hesitancy as doubt in disguise. His strategy, it seemed, was to keep firing religious questions until the response he got was a firm no rather than a gentle yes. As I recall, there were two prize questions that (in his mind) exposed our longsuffering host as a wicked heathen. Jackpot question one: "Before you take your child to school, do you pray to God to confirm that what you are doing is God's will?" Her: "Uh, no ..." Jackpot question two: "Do you pray to God before you go to the hair salon?" Timidity gave way to bafflement, and our host responded, "Well no! Why would I do that?" Our lead inquisitor pronounced that if she were in a right relationship with Jesus Christ, she would find out if it was God's will for her to do each task of her day. Time for repentance!

We prayed a prayer of confession. Our leader prayed for the host's salvation. Then we left.

When we arrived at the conference center's parking lot, we spotted the pastor whose church was sponsoring the event. Our leader bolted across the asphalt, grabbed his pastor, and proclaimed victoriously, "I got another one for the kingdom!"

I was aghast. I made a vow to God that day that I would never participate in anything like that again. I vowed to God that I would confront the perpetrator, apologize to the host, and take my leave. And I did.

A Peek at the Playbook

Everybody has an awkward evangelism story. Jeremy's story involves contact sports.

The man was tall and confident and radiated uncontainable energy. When he said he turned down a career in the NFL because God called him to be a traveling revival preacher, all the young men in the audience were electrified, wide-eyed, slack-jawed, and viscerally absorbed. All the young men, that is, except for me.

It was "Spiritual Emphasis Week" at our small Bible college, and I found myself in the unspiritual position of envying the rapture my fellow students were experiencing. I knew part of the problem was that the inherent connection between God and contact sports was somehow lost on me. Although my dad was and is a committed believer, a pillar in his church, and a faithful husband and father, he also preferred *Star Trek* to Sunday football. I wondered if he was somehow to blame.

About midweek, the revival preacher called us to a radical task: door-to-door, cold-call evangelism. We'd knock on doors, tell complete strangers about Jesus, and souls would be saved this very week. This very week! He'd done it all over the country! Get in the game! Again, I was in an awkward spot. I believed in Jesus, in evangelism, and in salvation, but for some reason, at age nineteen, I had doubts about the efficacy of this approach. I also had doubts about my doubts and wondered if I was simply an unfaithful, foot-dragging coward for not going along with the contagious momentum of it all.

My single courageous moment came when I approached the revival speaker in the student cafeteria. The young men around him were asking if he'd ever consider going back to the NFL. (Answer: no). With hesitation, I asked him a different question. "You lead students all over the country in door-to-door evangelism. Um, how much good does it actually do?"

He didn't even look up from his lunch tray. He held his fingers one-inch apart and replied, "About this much. We don't do it for them. We do it for us."

3

His honesty hit me like a blindside tackle. Before I had the presence of mind to clarify who he meant by "us" and "them," he continued. "Almost no one comes to believe in Jesus because of the cold-calling we do. So it's doesn't do much good for the non-Christians." Then he smiled. "The students who do the cold-calling, though, they get changed. It can be scary to share your faith, but those who do this kind of evangelism usually aren't scared after an experience like this. After this week, they'll be able to share their faith with anybody, anytime, so it does them a *lot* of good."

I had a few friends who did knock on the doors of strangers. I don't recall any victory reports or crisis conversions, which we all felt was a little disappointing, but the students still described it as a meaningful experience. When those doors opened, my friends met many people who were lonely, a few who were unsure of what they believed, and several who described themselves as Christians without a church home. They did develop a healthy confidence about sharing their faith, and I loved hearing their stories. I also wondered if it was best practice to rally young Christians to one goal ("Save the lost!") when the real goal, still good, was much less direct ("Personal enrichment!").

I didn't do the cold-calling, but that week changed me too.

Many conversations about evangelism begin and end with unfortunately true stories, stinging encounters with the silly, the inept, or the unethical. Perhaps you have a few tales you could tell. Or scars you could show. The people inside our churches—and outside—probably do too. But should the story end there?

We believe that the unfortunately true stories should be heard, studied, and learned from, but they should not be allowed to have the last word. We believe the good news is far better than the bad stories. Why should an unsavory encounter with a pushy preacher cause a resurrection faith to roll over and play dead? If the gospel is more powerful than sin and death, more powerful than hate and war, the gospel is also more powerful than the evangelistic disasters created by those who lay claim to it. Why should we surrender our hearts to a bad experience? Instead, we should ask, in faith and hope and love, "What is the more excellent way?"

For us, the more excellent way involves *relationships*.

Good Relationships + Good News

Relationships matter. Maybe this is old news to you, but it's taken us awhile to figure this out. Consider:

- From the beginning, the Bible is profoundly relational. For all the goodness of creation, God created both man and woman because to "be alone" is "not good" (Genesis 2:18). God walked and talked in the same paradise garden as Adam and Eve (Genesis 3:8). And it is the ruptured relationship and banishment from paradise that calls forth God's mission to restore a broken creation.
- Although it's not always recognized, so much of Scripture assumes connections: tribes, covenants, families, neighbors, even enemies. And if you remove the relational setting, many of the foundational truths of Christianity don't make sense. How do we begin to live or even understand things like forgiveness, love, reconciliation, and trust without relationships as a context?
- Jesus' ministry was profoundly relational. Not only was Jesus recognized—and criticized—as a "friend of sinners" (Matthew 11:19), Jesus also called his followers his friends (John 15:15).
- Followers of Jesus are called to be stewards of all things: our time, our money, talents, bodies, and the planet.

But when was last time you heard a sermon about being stewards of our relationships?

- Even the most sophisticated Christian theology is not just about abstract, disembodied ideas. It involves some kind of bond—of respect, mentoring, and guidance—between students and teachers. It might not be spelled out on the printed page, but the relationship is there, and it's crucial.

Christian discipleship does not exist in a relational vacuum. It never has. So what would happen if the invitation to discipleship were also profoundly relational?

Some folks call this practice "relational evangelism." We didn't invent the term, but here's how we mean it. By relational, we mean a genuine, ongoing, loving, give-and-take presence with other flesh-and-blood human beings. The bond may be deep, or it may be new, but the important thing is that the bond is real. By evangelism, we mean expressing the very good news about Jesus. Taken together, relational evangelism means opening up our lives and expressing our faith—implicitly and explicitly—with people who have no doubt that we care for them. It means initiating loving friendships because that's what Jesus did. And it means growing in God's grace all through the process.

This is not original. It was happening long before we got here, and it'll be happening long after we're gone from this earth. It's not a program, project, formula, or technique. It's not just for (insert denominational identity here), (insert theological tradition here), or (insert personality type, spiritual gift, or sociological category here). It's not just for experts. It's not just for Christians who are 100 percent sure about 100 percent of what they believe 100 percent of the time.

Labels abound. Some call this practice "friendship evangelism," "lifestyle evangelism," or "invitational evangelism."

Some call it "incarnational evangelism," believing this approach follows the "with us" nature of Jesus' incarnation. Others call it "hospitality evangelism" while still others just call it "biblical hospitality." We've heard the term "affinity outreach" as shared interests and experiences become the basis for natural faith sharing. One friend refers to it as "doing life together." And some people just call this "Christians making friends." We say use whatever term you like. We're flexible. We're not advocating a particular title; we're advocating a way of life and a practice of relating that contains certain things. And the contents matter more than the label.

Relational evangelism is a way of loving God and loving our neighbor. But, of course, this is hard to do if we're running from God or avoiding our neighbors.

What We Have ... and What We Don't

Whenever we talk to congregations about reaching out and sharing their faith, we often hear two back-to-back responses:

1. "Of course our church would like to grow! In fact, we need to."
2. "But we don't have (_____) that other churches do."

What our churches feel like they lack, i.e. what fills in the blank, ranges wildly. It can be a tool, asset, or strength, or some key to growth and vitality that others churches have or seem to have.

"Of course our church would like
to grow! But we don't have ...

- a new building or a hip venue."
- a big staff."
- a huge youth group that goes on expensive outings."
- a high population density in the community."
- people in the community who are interested in going to church."
- catchy mass mailings."
- the latest presentational technology for worship or teaching."
- a graphic artist in residence."
- a flashy website."
- dynamic musicians."
- cool hairdos."
- a media team that produces professional videos."
- a powerful social media campaign."
- a coffeehouse."
- top-notch children's play areas equipped with inflatable bouncy houses (and a good insurance plan)."
- hologram technology that beams the pastor, *Star Wars*-style, into multisite venues for the sermon."

In case you think we're kidding about that list, we're not. We know churches that have every one of these things. And we're not knocking the churches that do. We're happy for them! But (stay with us here) the truth is, more than a few of us are guilty of looking down our noses and making subtle sideswipes at other churches that have tools, assets, and strengths that our own congregations lack. We may cloak a critique in intellectual or theological terms, but we suspect that the roots of our criticism are well hidden. Deep in our hearts, we're envious. And even if we're not envious of the tool itself (say, hologram technology), we are often jealous of the results that seem to be associated with it.

So here's some good news: Friendship does not require hologram technology. Caring companionship does not require a big budget, graphic artists, or good hair (just ask us, we know about this one). And friendship can make the biggest difference in our lives, in the lives of others, in the life of our church, and for the sake of God's kingdom. Real-life human contact does not require tools.

But there is also bad news: we still resist making friends. This sounds crazy, but it's true. We can be hesitant—perpetually hesitant—about initiating connections with those we don't know. And even the relationships we do have, well, we're not always good at keeping those thriving and healthy. So the one thing that all of us can do—make friends—is the one thing we'll go to great lengths to avoid doing.

We know of one church on the East Coast whose members decided to reach out to their neighborhood. "But what does our neighborhood need?" they asked. So they formed a committee of smart, committed believers who decided to craft a survey for every household in the area. Potentially, this was a good move. But here's what happened:

Meeting #1:   The committee met and worked on the survey.

Meeting #2:   The committee met and worked on the survey some more.

Meeting #3:   The committee met, pored over the document, manicured the questions, and considered every possible angle on everything.

Meeting #47: The survey was now one million pages long (that might be an exaggeration). The survey also never saw the light of day, and the committee never connected with the community. Privately, the pastor came to a sobering conclusion, telling us, "I began to suspect that our real mission was

9

twofold: to talk among ourselves about outreach and to protect ourselves from ever having any real human contact beyond our small group. And we succeeded in that mission."

It's hard to come clean about this in polite company. It's easier to send out a mass mailing than it is to make a friend. It's easier to install a great sound system (or complain about churches that do) than it is to initiate meaningful interpersonal contact. It's easier to critique superficial relationships on Facebook than it is to build the authentic relationships we claim to be advocating. Our brothers and sisters who have opened fantastic coffeehouses as a labor of love and Christian service tell us opening a coffeehouse is a lot of work … but it may be easier than coming face-to-face with a very real, very complicated human being who, whether he or she realizes it or not, is searching for the face of God. Relationships are complicated, messy, awkward, unpredictable, hurtful, and time-intensive. Relationships put our hearts at risk, and because of this, they are not for the risk-averse. Deep down, we know this.

So maybe what our Christian communities are missing isn't just money, staff, buildings, or inflatable bouncy houses. Maybe what we're missing is something less tangible, less quantifiable. Something like interpersonal "oomph." Maybe we need to fess up and say, "Of course we would like our church to grow! In fact, we need to. But we don't have the *courage* to build new relationships."

Time for repentance?

It's probably easier for you to read one more book—even this book—than it is to risk your heart by reaching out to a stranger. The authors of this book will be the first to admit that it's more convenient for us to write this book than it is for us to do what it says. But at our best, we are all capable of courageous moments. We've done it before. And we'll tell you: *relational evangelism is risky but worth it.*

A (Fortunately) True Story

Jenni and Alexis were a study in contrasts. Jenni was short, sweet, and approachable, with a quick smile that put people at ease. Alexis, on the other hand, was overweight, overconfident, and intimidating, with a spiky hairdo and prominent facial scar. They worked in the same office.

One evening after working late, Jenni announced that she was calling it quits for the day. Alexis asked, "Where are you headed?"

"A church thing." Jenni had only spoken three words and without much thought, but now she realized that Alexis was quietly bristling.

After a few tense seconds, Alexis said, "I'm ... not sure I believe in that religion stuff." She tried sounding casual, but it wasn't working.

"Religion?" Jenni responded. "I don't have much faith in religion either. My faith is ... somewhere else." Sensing that Alexis had said all that she would say, Jenni smiled and left for her church event.

A door had opened, but a door leading to what? Both women wondered if they had contributed to an awkward work environment.

Cautiously, in the weeks that followed, a budding friendship began between the two women. When they occasionally ate lunch together, Alexis would make small, guarded inquiries into Jenni's faith, but mostly they just listened to each other. On days when Alexis was having an especially frustrating time at work, Jenni would try to boost her mood with short poems and Bible verses. She wasn't sure how Alexis would respond to the Bible verses, but soon Alexis began to return the favor.

Over a period of months, the bond grew and the exploration of faith along with it. Jenni invited Alexis to do a presentation about life skills at the afterschool program hosted by her church. An avid reader, Alexis bought a few Christian bestsellers (they were the easiest to find) and began journaling. Jenni bought Alexis a study Bible. Alexis even visited Jenni's church on a few irregular occasions, where she received a startlingly warm welcome.

Eventually, Alexis made a series of veiled confessions to Jenni. She carried within her a tremendous amount of shame for things she had done in her past. This burden affected her health, including her ability to get a good night's sleep. For her part, Jenni admitted to Alexis that she struggled with depression. By this point, the two women genuinely cared for each other and relied on each other for encouragement.

Over a period of two years, Alexis felt comfortable enough to ask Jenni hard questions about God, the Bible, forgiveness, and suffering. Jenni listened well and offered sound answers, but they were never good enough for Alexis. Over time, Jenni began to detect that there was an ache in Alexis that would never be soothed by answers, no matter how biblically accurate they were. Jenni suggested that Alexis talk to her pastor, who was both knowledgeable and compassionate. Alexis and the pastor met for dinner, but Alexis squandered the time, making silly jokes and being evasive.

One evening, after a short shopping trip together, Alexis and Jenni stayed up late talking about their lives. Jenni's husband had gone to bed hours earlier, and rather than face the long drive to her home late at night, Alexis asked to sleep on the couch in the couple's basement. She took a book, her study Bible, and her journal. That night, the words in Alexis's journal were directed to God. "I am still pretty sure that I am unlovable. But I also know I have been avoiding you. I don't want to avoid you anymore. I will say yes to you."

I wish I could tell you that Alexis's life was immediately smoother, and that her openness to God brought an endless stream of sweatless victories her way. I wish I could tell you that her suffocating shame disappeared forever. But I can't.

What I can tell you is that the next morning, Alexis sheepishly informed her bleary-eyed hosts that she had decided to follow Jesus. I can tell you she was immediately welcomed into Jenni's church. And I can tell you that in the sanctuary of a friendly home, that night she slept like a baby.

Chapter 2

UNPACKING RELATIONAL EVANGELISM

My wife can make magic happen with a suitcase. For her, packing is a serious game of three-dimensional Tetris, and she wins by stuffing our luggage to maximum capacity. Opening one of her compact, geometric masterpieces becomes a clown-car exercise, where an implausible quantity of content spills out in all directions. From the outside, it looks like a tidy valise, but it holds far, far more than it appears.

Relational evangelism is a tidy term, but it, too, contains far more than it appears. In the spirit of unpacking this vital spiritual practice, here are seven things that relational evangelism is and does:

1. Relational evangelism is the stewardship of both content and context.

In this sense, context refers to a relational environment, a friendship. The good news about Jesus is that he is not a disembodied, abstract concept. Rather, if we believe John 14:6, "the Truth is a person." We're not sure who coined that phrase, but we like it.

Salt and light (Matthew 5:13–16) requires contact in order to demonstrate their potency, and relationships that are seasoned and brightened will make a case for Christ that transcends argument. We demonstrate the faith by sharing our life. (For more practical tips on how to do this, see Chapter 4, "Learning Hospitality"; Chapter 5, "Making Friends"; and Chapter 6, "Inviting People.")

But content matters as well, and by this we mean a verbal, respectful, gentle explanation for the hope we have (1 Peter 3:15). We know of one community ministry that delivers food to hungry people. Their motto and mission is "Serve until they ask why," and they have a strict policy of not talking about their faith unless asked. This effort is excellent, but those who have led this work for decades recently confessed, "Over all these years, almost no one has asked us why."

Sadly, this ministry is about to close. We're not saying that all Christians should have all the answers, but all of us should have enough to say for people to understand the connection between our faith and our acts of kindness. (For more practical tips on how to do this, see Chapter 7, "Finding Words.")

Depending on our personalities, theological traditions, or biases, most of us tend toward hospitable connecting (context) or verbal faith sharing (content). But if we are stewards of all that we have, this means we are stewards of both our words and our deeds. This holy trust calls us beyond our personalities, theological traditions, and biases. The tandem practice of both language and lifestyle helps us avoid lopsided tendencies and creates an integrated, non-compartmentalized faith. God's power is made known when God's people have the integrity to demonstrate an abundant quality of life and the courage to name its source.

2.   Relational evangelism isn't transactional.

Transactional may feel like a clumsy word, but consider that much of our life is based on the reality of transactional relationships—tit for tat, this for that, quid pro quo. I give money to my barista, and she gives me coffee—a commercial transaction. I take someone out for lunch this week, and next week, he or she returns the favor—a social transaction. We do this all the time without even thinking about it.

In fact, to not follow this transactional pattern can be rude at best and illegal at worst. My barista doesn't have to love me or even like me (nor I her), but if I give her five dollars, I'm entitled to my latte. That's how transactions work.

Relational evangelism is not like this. In fact, relational evangelism is rooted in *agape*, and part of the radical notion of agape is unconditional love. Agape is a love given without condition, requirement, or obligation of return from the other party. There is no catch. Agape is non-transactional love rather than a loveless transaction.

Transactional relating corrupts Christian love. Relating to others in a way that quietly (or conspicuously) keeps score devitalizes our witness. Our Christian service should not put someone else in our debt—one they repay by doing obligatory things like coming to church or talking about God. This transaction is little more than spiritual bribery. Two stories illustrate its long history and real danger.

First, I own a small collection of antique beads called padre beads. If I have the story right, Spanish missionaries, monks, and friars in the early colonial days of America used these small, blue baubles. These priests found that Native Americans didn't like attending Mass, but they did love beads. So the priests worked out a deal. If they attended Mass, they gave them beads afterward. No Mass, no beads.

As a transaction, it worked. Natives showed up for Mass as long as the beads were provided. But a transaction isn't the same thing as a transformation.

Second, I was recently invited to speak with a group of committed, energetic, and multinational Christian college students who volunteered to work with refugees arriving in the United States. As I was sharing about non-transactional hospitality, one woman became visibly upset. Unable to contain herself, she blurted out, "The transaction thing! I do that! I spend a lot of time having refugees over to my home to eat. I do this to show hospitality and share my faith. But after a few meals, I get mad because they haven't become Christians yet. I've even grown bitter toward them. God has been showing me that my resentment is a sign that something is wrong, but I didn't know what. Now I know. Without even thinking it through, I felt that my hospitality entitled me to their conversion. And I know I can't do that anymore."

Her confession was spontaneous, urgent, and lacked self-consciousness. Also, the others around the table deeply supported it.

It takes a great deal of courage to crucify our sense of entitlement. Invite without obligating. Share without keeping score. Christian discipleship means we owe Jesus everything and nobody owes us anything.

3.   Relational evangelism is gradually facilitated work.

Consider the Bible passages about evangelism or discipleship that use agrarian metaphors. Our favorite is the parable of the sower, found in three places in the Bible (Mark 4:1–20; Matthew 13:1–23; Luke 8:1–15). But many Americans are disconnected from our own farming practices, let alone the farming practices of biblical times. We aren't farm-food people; we're fast-food people. So an abbreviated agricultural reeducation is probably in order. Following are just three points:

First, it's hard to put farming in fast-forward. Tending the soil requires consistency, steadiness, and regularity, and compost is best when turned daily. This fits perfectly with Christian evangelism and discipleship, as consistent attentiveness, steady kindness, and the repetitious demonstration of concern can add up to a verdant, fertile witness. But this is a slow accumulation and a gradual process by nature.

Second, it's remarkably hard to make your garden grow. In fact, we can't force growth in much of anything, but we can facilitate it. We note the seasons, attend to the conditions, and nurture the potential for fruitfulness. Again, this is a natural description of Christian evangelism and discipleship. One does not coerce the harvest.

Third, it's labor. A photo of a pretty garden on a magazine cover only shows a fraction of the true picture. The sore back, sweat rings, and perennially dirty fingernails are conveniently cropped out. Wrenching stones and yanking weeds are all part of making good ground, but such work is work. Note that while Jesus said, "The harvest is plentiful," he also decried a distinct shortage of "laborers" (Matthew 9:37; Luke 10:2). Perhaps a new emphasis should be placed on the holy sweat and unglamorous faithfulness that defines such labor.

There are two dangers at play here. The first danger is to ignore the legitimately biblical alternatives to the agrarian metaphors. In Acts 2:14–41, Peter preaches a short confrontational message and three thousand are saved in a single day. This is true, and we love it. But it's also true that we aren't Peter. (Further, we have found that sometimes those who favor confrontational approaches can be impatient at best and seeking proof texts to excuse their bad social skills at worst.)

The second danger comes into play when we appear willing to delay gratification. By gratification, we mean the results of our efforts for Christian evangelism and discipleship. We've heard church leaders say, "You may never see the fruit." On the surface, this sounds like a quote from the Bible and makes a valid point. But the reality is that sometimes we do not see fruit because our hand is not on the plow. In this case, we haven't delayed gratification; we have only delayed evaluation. We may never see the fruit, but if none ever comes, we'll be known by that too (Matthew 7:20; Luke 6:44).

4. Relational evangelism corrects overcorrection.

It's our conviction that the worst evangelistic approaches are manipulative, unkind, and do more harm than good. But it's also our conviction that evangelistic reticence is not the answer either. Here's what we mean. Are there dishonest, abusive, bloodsucking charlatans who abuse others in the name of Christian evangelism? Yes. Does this cause many of us non-bloodsuckers to shrink back in horror? Yes.

And does our shrinking back sometimes extend to the point where we are reticent (at least) or unwilling (at most) to share our faith at all? If we're honest, for many of us the answer is yes.

But reticence is not reform; it doesn't correct anything. In fact, our perpetual reserve can become a phobic, counterproductive overcorrection. We have heard these words from the lips of believing people we know and love: "I have no interest in evangelism, because evangelists are just religious scalp collectors." Or "Not only do I avoid evangelism, I won't even use the word *evangelism*. That way, others don't associate us with them." Or "The most faithful, Christlike thing I can do is serve a person, not twist his or her arm into believing what I believe."

The ironic thing about this kind of perspective is that it begins with righteous indignation and ends in self-righteousness. We say, "I don't want to be like *that!*" and drift gradually backward into an untenable position where we are convinced that the most faithful thing to do is the opposite of what Jesus actually said to do—make disciples. Of course, we shouldn't coerce people into believing what we believe. But the hard truth is that if sincere believers give up on evangelism, we become part of the problem. If we opt out of faith sharing in any real form, we are handing the whole business over to the bloodsuckers, and we are enabling the abuse by not providing an alternative. And relational evangelism is one alternative. (If you still have your doubts about faith sharing, check out Chapter 3, "Reluctant Evangelists.")

5. Relational evangelism is reparative.

By reparative we mean "mending," "renovating," or "restoring." To this end, relational evangelism recognizes two things. The first is that for some people, the deepest obstacles to Christian discipleship are very often our deepest pains: betrayal, broken-heartedness, harm that others have done to us, or shame for the harm we have done to others. Second, relational evangelism recognizes the dynamic recently shared with us by a friend: "What was broken in relationship must be repaired in relationship."

For example, consider the reality of childhood sexual abuse. Experts say that approximately one in four women and one in five men are victims of childhood sexual abuse. (Please put this book down for a moment and consider the souls behind that statistic. Please.) Abuse wreaks havoc on trust, and such a profound betrayal can damage a person's ability or willingness to meaningfully depend on others. Now consider the fact that trust—specifically, trusting the Lord—is nonnegotiably central to Christianity. What then? The person who has experienced a trust-shattering trauma will very often need to find a single person worthy of his or her trust before they can consciously trust anyone or anything else. Even if a person is not a trauma victim, he or she may need to have a personal relationship with a trustworthy Christian (a "little Christ") as a stepping-stone to finally consciously, meaningfully depend on Christ (and Christ alone).

Healthy relationships rehabilitate us. And interpersonal connections that bring good news into our lives can be the means by which we are reconciled to God and others. To clarify, it is Christ who saves. Christ is Lord, not us. But this saving Lord has chosen human agents, as "we are ambassadors for Christ ... God is making his appeal through us" (2 Corinthians 5:20). And part of the role of the ambassador is the diplomatic mission of building, or rebuilding, bridges that lead to the kingdom.

6.   Relational evangelism is mutually transforming.

The church is the body of Christ, the hands and feet of Jesus in this world. But as members of this peculiar corpus, we've often questioned the efficiency of God's strategy. If it's easier to do it yourself, why does God delegate? Why would God choose dull tools like us? If God truly has unlimited options, why such a seemingly indirect approach?

The answer came, of all places, in a sermon on Christian financial stewardship. The pastor said, "The truth about tithing is that God does not need your money. He never has. The truth about tithing is not a God who needs to receive but a people who need to give. Generosity does not change God. It changes us."

Can this also relate to faith sharing? The same Christ who said, "Go and make disciples," also said, "It is more blessed to give than to receive" (Acts 20:35). One of the most disappointing misconceptions about Christian evangelism is that it is a one-way street and a one-way conversation. But in relational evangelism, nothing could be further from the truth. Of course, "faith comes by hearing" (Romans 10:17), but as disciples of Jesus, our faith also grows in the telling. Educators know that it is the teachers who learn the most. So will Jesus, our Rabbi, not teach us as we teach others? Will Jesus, our Immanuel, not be with us as we seek to be with others?

A woman we'll call Nancy is a middle-aged, reserved, dutiful children's Sunday school teacher in the southwestern United States. In every single season of her life, Nancy has been steeped in the faith and in the church. One Sunday, as a result of her church's efforts to reach out to the neighborhood, a gap-toothed, red-haired, nine-year-old girl abruptly appeared in Nancy's Sunday school class. The little girl had had no contact of any kind with any church, and Nancy soon found that her new pupil's biblical knowledge was absolute zero.

Sunday's class went fairly well, but that evening, Nancy's husband was startled to find his wife driven to her knees in tearful prayer. In the months that followed, Nancy looked forward to teaching Sunday school in a way she never had before. Always a faithful preparer,

Nancy now readied her lessons with vigor and her expectations for total bewilderment from her newest student. The little girl's hyperactivity and horrible home life contributed to behavioral problems, but most Sundays, Nancy was more than a match for her. Without seeking it, Nancy experienced an unusually raw closeness to the Lord that was not the result of reading another book, attending another Bible study, or signing up for another retreat.

There are several powerful things about this true story, but we'll point out only two. The first is that it shatters the stereotype of faith sharing as a one-way experience, where the convert changes and the evangelist escapes unscathed and unchanged. Nancy's experience isn't unusual in this respect. Relational evangelism unleashes two-way blessings. The second thing, ironically, is that Nancy would never describe herself as an evangelist. In fact, she would politely but firmly tell you that evangelism makes her uncomfortable and is something she has never done even once in her entire life. But by taking a cantankerous little girl under her wing and sharing with her the most basic Bible lessons, evangelism is exactly what Nancy was doing, and it changed them both. Sometimes the task also sharpens the tool. (Just don't tell Nancy.)

7.   It works, but it takes practice.

We know of one study that contrasted growing churches with churches that were plateaued or declining. You can get the details in the chart below, but here is the bottom line:

Growing Churches (Group A)
have many members who ARE comfortable talking about their faith and are simply inviting people to worship and other activities.

Plateaued or Declining Churches (Group B)
have many members who are NOT comfortable talking about their faith and are NOT simply inviting people to worship and other activities.

This study was repeated four times in twenty years and involved churches of many different denominational traditions and geographical settings. The figures reported here are from the 2008 study and involve 408 congregations from 12 denominations, though results have been fairly consistent each time the study has been conducted. Source: Christian Community.

The percentages below denote those who *agreed* with the statement.

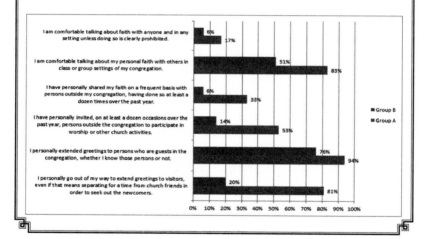

Think about the significance of this:

- **Only 14 percent** of those in plateaued or declining congregations (Group B) **are frequently inviting** someone to attend church activities.
- **Only 6 percent** of those in such congregations are **frequently sharing their faith** with persons outside the church.
- When visitors do come to those declining churches, **80 percent of the congregation will not leave a conversation with church friends** to seek out the visitor and greet them.

It's time for a gut check. Many people think they know how to welcome visitors and practice hospitality. But most of us, as individuals and as churches, are not as friendly as we think we are. Both hard studies and personal experience bear this out.

So how do we move our congregations from Group B to Group A? When the same respondents were asked if they had been offered some kind of training in faith sharing and inviting, this was the response:

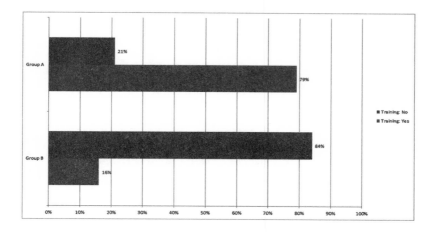

Training is the game-changer.

Sharing the faith is spiritual, but it isn't magical. It takes time, training, coaching, and practice. It requires the discipline of discipleship. And it takes the willingness to *learn* and the willingness to *do.*

Chapter 3

RELUCTANT EVANGELISTS

If you consider yourself an expert evangelist, skip this chapter. But if you're uncomfortable sharing your faith and are reading this book in spite of yourself, congratulations! This chapter is for you. We've heard a few objections from Christians who are pretty sure that faith sharing isn't for them. And we think those qualms, questions, hang-ups, and baggage should be explored, not ignored. So in no particular order, this chapter addresses twenty objections for one simple reason: we are convinced that *reluctant evangelists can be the best evangelists.*

"I'm an introvert, not an extrovert."

It's true that most don't associate evangelism with people who are reserved, quiet, timid, or shy. But this is an experiential association, not a biblical one. An effusive overtalker does not an evangelist make. This is especially true in relational faith sharing, which often involves generous amounts of nondefensive listening. And in the context of a relationship, the so-called evangelist who is addicted to the sound of his or her own voice will soon be known for who he or she really is—a self-promoter rather than a Jesus-promoter.

Of this book's authors, Fred is an introvert who is often mistaken for an extrovert. Jeremy is a helpless extrovert who happens to relish solitude. And both of us say that our character traits can (and should) shape *how* we share our life and our faith, but they shouldn't determine *if* we share our life and our faith. Evangelism is not a function of personality.

"I don't want others to feel pressured."

This is a principled concern. We're not asking you to force anything on anybody. But let's talk for a moment about pressure.

In his book *Conspiracy of Kindness*, Steve Sjogren shared how his view of faith sharing began in a personal pressure-cooker. "I felt bad about not being more effective in leading others to Christ, but whenever I did try to do evangelism, I would take on *unbearable responsibility for the outcome*" (emphasis added). Since he was feeling the heat himself, he began turning the temperature up for others. But the steam was released when he realized that "We don't carry the pressure for success in evangelism on our own shoulders." Instead, the Holy Spirit does. When we internalize this, he writes, "We can begin seeing ourselves as coworkers with the Holy Spirit ... our role is to *enjoy* the flow of God's life through us as we share our joy with others."

Does relational faith sharing require intentionality? Of course. Effort? Most relationships do. But pressure? No way. Pressure kills friendships, and our need to control outcomes by pressuring others only reveals our lack of faith in the power of the Holy Spirit.

"I don't have the answers for sophisticated theological questions, and I'm not into debates."

We dig civil debates, and we love higher education, but it is a misnomer that the most effective evangelists are learned theologians or able arguers. Rather, it's our experience that caring friendship usually trumps expertise.

Darren was an angry young man I met through our church's outreach ministries. He came across as unbelieving and unafraid, and when he asked me to meet with him at Taco Bell to discuss his hard questions about Christianity, I was thrilled. I had just taken a course in Christian apologetics and was eager to give a vigorous and rational defense of the faith. But after a solid hour of livid inquiry from Darren, he suddenly bolted from our table and went home. His monologue had allowed no space for me to respond. I was dejected, certain I had somehow failed. The next day, he called me and with relief in his voice said, "Thanks for answering my questions. I want to know more."

This did not compute. I had offered zero answers. Since Darren's objections to Jesus were couched in rational terms, I assumed his barriers to believing were rational. They weren't.

There are people who will want to engage in serious intellectual wrestling before they choose to believe in Jesus. But one pastor we know says that less than 10 percent of people fit into this category. In our experience, it's much less than that. You're not a Jeopardy-caliber Christian apologist? Don't worry. It's okay. Besides, what is the body of Christ for? If you meet an intense seeker who demands expert-level responses to his or her questions, refer him or her to an expert (Like your pastor! Put that seminary degree to use!). But don't let what you cannot offer stop you from offering what you can—friendship.

"I can't talk about my faith because it's too personal a topic, like sex or money."

Sexuality, personal finance, and faith are personal topics and not usually the stuff of conversation between strangers. Think about it: When was the last time you walked up to someone you didn't know and began talking about earned income potential or asked, "If you were to be audited today, where would you go?" And sex with strangers? No way. Random intimacy is a perversion.

But we're not preaching closeness without context. Invest in meaningful connections, and talk about things that matter, including what you believe. If my relationship with Christ has infused my life, and if I share my life with others, sharing about Christ can come naturally. In fact, such sharing would be conspicuous in its absence. Are our friendships so fragile they cannot bear the weight of substantive dialogue? Personal conversations are the stuff of personal relationships.

Choose your friends wisely, but do not allow yourself to be trapped by the safely impersonal topics of sports and weather. Make friends, talk about things that matter, and make it personal.

"I don't believe in altar calls."

Once while waiting in a long line, I struck up a conversation with the woman next to me. She asked me what I did for a living. I'm a pastor, and I have learned that the unveiling of my vocation to a stranger usually triggers love, hate, or uneasiness from the person who popped the question. In this case, I said "I'm a pastor," and she was delighted. My status elevated (temporarily), she asked many excited questions about my work. At one point, she said giddily, "I'll bet you do altar calls all the time!" Sensing that my answer could disappoint, I took a deep breath and replied that while I had no problem with altar calls, I did not happen to use them. She was aghast. Her eyes widened, and she physically drew back before asking suspiciously, "Don't you believe in salvation?"

I couldn't explain to this sister that the architecture of our sanctuary did not lend itself to worshippers approaching the altar, even for prayer. And I didn't see the use in pointing out that Christian salvation very much predates altar calls, a recent ritual that originally began as a way to collect signatures for the abolition of slavery. Our setting, along with her mercurial regard, precluded teachability. So I'll share with you what I couldn't share with her. Too many of us have fused evangelism with a particular evangelistic approach. Altar calls (or tracts or radio ads or flannel graphs or …) do not equal evangelism. We believe firmly that means and ends and efficacy are all important, so do what you believe in and do what works. But don't allow one particular method to separate you from seeking a godly goal.

"I don't feel like our church has anything to offer certain groups of people."

We hear this most often from churches with few people under age forty. We also hear it occasionally when there is a major demographic discrepancy between church and community, like when a well-educated Anglo congregation finds itself in a working-class Latin neighborhood. This sensitivity is legitimate, and we'd offer three things to consider.

First, be aware of what you do have. A social worker we'll call Tyrone belonged to a small congregation in the Northwest that was in the process of revitalizing. One Sunday after worship, Tyrone, disappointed, approached his pastor and said, "I want my son to come with me to church, but he's in his mid-thirties. I look around, and there's no one here his age." His pastor glanced around the room and replied, "We had about seventy people in worship today. About a dozen of them are your son's age, but none of those folks are in the sanctuary. Most of them help with the children's ministries located in other parts of the building. So you might not see them, but they're here." Take more than a cursory look at the people in your congregation's network. You might be surprised.

Second, offer who you really are and bring God into it. Early in my time at one struggling congregation, a woman no one knew appeared in worship. A single mom with a deep faith and a heart for ministry, she was trying to decide if we could be a spiritual home for her. But our church was bereft of teens, so what would her daughter do?

I met with the woman for coffee. I wanted so badly for this family to connect with our congregation, but I knew I wouldn't respect myself if I donned a desperate smile and faked optimism. After hearing her concerns, I said, "We are a turnaround church. I hate to put it this way, but if you're looking for a strong congregation with a full menu of programs, we're probably not the church for you. We have fifteen people in worship. Our sanctuary has orange shag carpet that smells funny. But we are building something, and we are here because we believe God wants us to be here. If you feel like God wants you to be a part of a transformation, this might be the church for you."

I learned a lesson at that moment: Do not underestimate the integrity of simply saying who you are. If pastors stop acting like salesmen, perhaps parishioners will stop acting like customers, and discernment will trump consumer impulses. For the person seeking a church home, the question "What does God want me to do?" is probably better than the question "What can this church do for me?"

Third, start something! Your church may lack critical mass in certain demographic groups, but recognizing this is the first step in doing something about it. Make a concerted effort, expect a degree of failure, and resolve to learn from it. Recruit others, throw a party, and cast the net wide. Invite five or six or seven times as many people as you'd like to see come. If it looks like no one will show up, read Luke 14:16–24 and invite "the poor, the crippled, the blind, and the lame" ... or just invite them to start with! Your efforts and the Spirit's help might fill the gap, or it might take you in a new and unexpected direction.

"Isn't it selfish to share our faith in order for our church to grow?"

We know of one small, gifted congregation in the Southwest who found itself on an unsustainable trajectory. They cherished the familial bond within their body of believers, but membership decline signaled trouble ahead. We were impressed with the astute church board chairperson who said, "The people who are here are my family. But *I want my family to grow.*"

It's selfish to operate a religious bait-and-switch scheme, where the blessing of the gospel is the bait and the burden of a sagging institution is the switch. A church might preach "Jesus saves!" while secretly praying that newcomers will come and save the church (without changing it). That's selfish. But it's not selfish to want your family—or God's family—to grow.

"I don't want our church to be a mega-church."

Although there is no absolute rule, most experts consider a mega-church to be a congregation of about two thousand or more in average worship attendance. Our perspective is that there is nothing wrong with being a mega-church or not being a mega-church. But the irony is that the protestation "We don't want to be a mega-church" seems to especially come from churches who run zero risk of being such. We've heard this concern tearfully expressed by churches with less than twenty people in average worship attendance. That's not a mega-church; that's a *micro*-church. Even a fellowship of two hundred is a long way from the "mega" category. We'd respectfully suggest that the obvious unreality of this objection is probably rooted in some kind of fear. This fear should not be allowed to stifle a Christ-centered, community-building vision of faith sharing and hospitality.

"We aren't concerned about being fruitful. We just want to be faithful."

This sentiment is legion. We hear it from churches, educational institutions, and books and periodicals. We hear it from pastors and laypeople. But we don't hear it from Scripture or, oddly enough, from farmers. This is because neither the Bible nor the farm put fruitfulness and faithfulness in opposing categories. They belong together. Try growing juicy summer tomatoes (fruitfulness) without consistent watering (faithfulness).

So why is this intrinsically illogical statement so prolific? We suspect there is a comparison game going on. Smaller ministries often feel inadequate next to larger ministries, so the temptation for the smaller ministry is to scramble for the moral high ground. Words like *fruitfulness* and *faithfulness* sound vaguely biblical, but such poetry often boils down to a brute comparison: "They may be the *bigger* church, but we're the *better* Christians." This is silly, and when spoken plainly, it reveals that the speaker might not possess the maturity he or she claims.

Are there people who seem to bypass God entirely and make an idol of large, popular, and apparently successful ministries? Yes. Is something healthy just because it grows? Not at all. Weeds grow. Tumors grow. And church size has never been an absolute measure of Christian faithfulness. But how we respond to feelings of inadequacy is a telling spiritual barometer. We often hide our disdain beneath a painfully thin layer of self-justification and religious language. Contempt is not the antidote for fandom, smugness is not an improvement on someone else's idolatry, and faithfulness is not the opposite of fruitfulness.

"I don't feel good about my church and/ or my pastor and/or my denomination."

We believe that following Jesus is a team sport and a group project and is best practiced in the imperfect community known as the church. At its best, the local congregation is part of the very body of Christ on Earth, an extended family of faith united by the radical grace and forgiveness of God. At its worst, of course, the church can be so self-absorbed, self-righteous, and self-seeking that it needs the radical grace and forgiveness of God as much as (or more than) anyone else. Pastors, churches, and denominations are all deeply flawed. So this one is hard.

If a person walked up to either Fred or Jeremy and said they were very unhappy with their church family, the questions we might ask are "Why are you unhappy? Why do you feel as you do? What experiences have brought these feelings about? Who have you talked with about this?" Then we'd listen a lot. If we were feeling a little gutsy, we might ask, "What would it take for you to feel good about your church, pastor, or denomination? What is really standing in the way of your wholehearted commitment?" Then we'd listen a lot more. And if we were feeling really bold, we might ask, "Although this is counterintuitive, how can your experience of discontent draw you closer to Christ?" Then they might walk away or tear up our preacher's card or something. But we mean it. If this describes you, ask God's Spirit to search your heart about this. Reflect on your discontent, and you might be surprised at the results.

- One woman told us she didn't feel good about the behavior of the teens in her church's youth group. But later, after thinking about it, she confessed that her unhappiness was rooted in her own perfectionism and control issues.
- One young man picked a fight with his pastor, who he felt was a theological lightweight. While not a fistfight, it was an unfruitful and prolonged conflict. Very late in the process, the instigator discovered that the real problem was his own pride, and that he needed to abandon his view of himself as the lonely enforcer of theological purity.
- We have a few friends who describe their church home in terms of seasons: there are dry seasons and verdant seasons,

highs and lows. When they reflect on their discontent, they often rediscover that sticking it out in all seasons is what they are called to do.

- As Christians, we say we believe in forgiveness. But our discontent may lead us to an unexpected realization, namely that we need to forgive the very people who taught us about forgiveness: our pastor, church, or denominational family.
- We know some who have come to the mature conclusion that they needed to "disagree and commit" rather than passively resist the direction their faith community was heading.
- There are those have an incompatible, different vision for ministry than their pastor, church, or denomination. Principled differences exist.
- At worst, there are those who have had such a toxic experience that it is in fact best for them to seek a healthier community.

I (Jeremy) used to pastor a church that had the only playground in town. And because it was open to the community, neighborhood families would often bring their kids for playdates and picnics. Recognizing this as an opportunity to reach out, I always tried to walk across the parking lot and chat with the families who dropped by. If the weather was nice, I'd talk with ten people a day. I learned to tell, with 100 percent accuracy, who already had a church home and who did not. Actually, their complaining made it easy. Those who already had a church home leaped at the chance to tell me everything that was wrong with it.

Some people switch churches like they switch TV channels, and to us, that's a sign of immaturity. But we also know too many local churches that are hamstrung by an ambivalent membership; they don't feel good enough about things to make a go of it, but they don't feel bad enough to leave. Again, we're not advocating church-hopping. And we believe that principled dissenters within a body should be respected. But why should our belonging be a cause for constant complaint? As a last resort, we ought to ask ourselves: Would my civil departure be doing my family, church, pastor, denomination or me a favor?

"I'm a Christian, but I'm not sure about everything I believe. What if it's unorthodox or just plain wrong?"

This can be a conscientious question. The question we would ask in response would be: What will you do with your uncertainty? How can you be a steward of your uncertainty? Here are three possibilities.

First, do not let your uncertainty freeze your witness. Offer the light you have. It may be more adequate than it feels to you.

Second, let the uncertainty about what you believe drive you deeper into Scripture, deeper into understanding Christianity for yourself, and deeper into mature discipleship. Feel like you don't know enough? You might be right. So learn! Grow! Don't be afraid that inquiry will expose your ignorance. Be afraid that ignorance will be used as an excuse for perpetual inaction.

Third, let the *awareness* of your *unawareness* be an asset. One of my professors used to say, "The greater the radius of our knowledge, the larger the circumference of our ignorance." Stephen Hawking famously said, "The greatest enemy of knowledge is not ignorance. It is the illusion of knowledge." By all means, develop your walk with the Lord however you can. Shun lazy minimalism. But remember that a healthy respect for what we don't know can be what keeps us humble.

"I am going through a real crisis. My faith feels so weak I can hardly imagine sharing it."

This is understandable. In fact, we wished we didn't understand this, but we do. Firsthand.

The year 2012 was bad for both of us. Really bad. We'll not bother with all the details, but at one point in 2012, one of Jeremy's friends said, "Dude, you're like Job." Of all the biblical characters I want to be compared to, Job is pretty low on my list. So if you are holding this book and in the midst of a difficult time, I guess the best thing we can say is thank you. And praise God. The fact that you're even considering any of this right now is a wonder to us. We also want you to know that we have prayed especially for you. We know what it is to be in crisis, including a crisis of faith. As we've strained ourselves onto these pages and written this book in a season of struggle, we have also poured out prayers for those who will read this book in a season of struggle. So even if we don't know you, we've been praying for you, and we hope that's worth something.

When we walk through the valley, we cannot take our cues from those who claim that the best Christian witness is constant and unwavering victory. These well-meaning folks may simply have baptized their denial. Pretend strength is no match for honest struggle. We must turn instead to Scripture. We'll find a great deal more than people coping with a bad day; much of Scripture is a case study of people in crisis. The slavery of the Hebrews. The death wishes of Elijah and Jonah. The haunted sleeplessness in the Psalms. The lamentations of Jeremiah. The cross. The Bible is filled with agonizing stories of people who are barely holding on. It's not pretty. But at the core of this desperate faith is the paradoxical relationship between weakness and strength and the nearness of God in the midst of crushing brokenheartedness.

Sister, brother, share what scraps you can. In Christ, it has more value and more power than you know. Lead with your own weakness and emptiness. Death does not have to have the last word.

"I take the peace, justice, and service emphasis of my church seriously. Sometimes I feel like there is a conflict between that and evangelism."[1]

For some of us, this is a big deal. Others may have no idea what we're referring to. Like most conflicts, this one is complicated. So before we address it, here's our attempt to explain it.

We all have different strengths and weaknesses, specialties and priorities, pet peeves and pet projects. This applies to individuals of all types and groups of all sizes. At best, this confluence of traits shapes our identity, even our calling from God, so it's important. We know entire denominations that excel at music production, for example, and we think that's part of their communal identity, part of why God put them on Earth.

But there is also a dark side. At our worst, we are tempted to make inflated value judgments about our relative strengths. In general terms, it sounds like "Real Christians focus on (insert *my* strengths here), not (insert *your* strengths here)." It's one thing to reflect our unique, God-given giftedness. It's another thing to compare and compete.

---

[1] There are many people who have shaped our thinking on this question, and here we acknowledge our debt to the writing of Leo Hartshorn and Dr. Darrell Guder. Some of Guder's work can be found here http://justiceunbound.org/journal/current-issue/evangelism-and-justice/ and some of Hartshorn's work can be found here http://www.mennonitemission.net/SiteCollectionDocuments/Tools%20for%20Mission/Missio%20Dei/MissioDei04.E.pdf

So how does this relate to faith sharing? Some churches, due to their history, theology, and calling, are known for excellence in evangelism. Others, for similar reasons, are known for an emphasis on peace, justice, and service. And the two groups don't always play nice with each other. In fact, they often view each other with suspicion and disdain.

In the Bible, we read that evangelism and justice are not mutually exclusive. But in the church we love, we hear this tragic refrain, "*Real* Christians focus on spreading the gospel, not saving the world." Or, "*Real* Christians focus on making peace, not making converts." We're ashamed to admit how many times we've heard this, and from people we really respect.

Too many Christians are playing for the same team but competing against each other. Leo Hartshorn asked, "Have evangelism and mission become the 'Jacob' and 'Esau' of church practice?" In some circles, the answer is yes, and that's very bad news, because it disintegrates the body of Christ. Dr. Darrell Guder identifies two major factions: one that groups itself around evangelism and another around social justice. Once the conflict takes on a life of its own, he writes, all parties "feed off stereotypes of each other." It is a sad irony when those who preach reconciliation with God and those who preach reconciliation with people both choose, publically or privately, to be at odds with each other.

We'll speak for ourselves and say that we want to be part of a rediscovery, a movement that inches toward merging these priorities and defactionalizing the body of Christ. Last time we checked, we need each other. Advocates for Christian peacemaking and advocates for Christian evangelism should not require the other camp to be the enemy. Sharing the good news does not have to be ideological colonialism, and ministries of justice and service do not have to elevate peace above God. Hartshorn says poignantly, "Mission without peace is salvation without ethics. And peace without mission is ethics without salvation."

"I don't know what to say. I don't know what words to use."

We think this is so important that we've devoted an entire chapter to it (see Chapter 7, "Finding Words"). But for now we'll say this: the word-search can become a God-search. That is, the effort to articulate our faith can in itself be something that builds our faith.

"I don't have friends who aren't already members of a church."

Longtime members and veteran disciples often find this to be true. It's both a social irony and a systematic problem. Our schedules are filled with Christian activities, and our social circles are populated by church friends. Our activity makes us unavailable, and we don't even realize it. If this describes you, perhaps it's worth asking some questions.

Do we really need to commit to another committee meeting? To the reliable soul, this might sound like betrayal, but we think the opposite might be true, especially if your church is operating with an unnecessarily large organizational system. We know of one congregation whose bylaws required a twenty-five-member governing board, but this same congregation had only twenty people in average worship attendance. While most of our attendance-to-board ratios are not so clownishly disproportionate, many of our congregations have structures that are no longer size-appropriate. When this is the case, "filling the slots" actually takes people away from the opportunity to form meaningful relationships with the spiritual seekers they know. What would happen if you quit one church meeting a month and instead took the initiative to meet at the local diner with one person you know who needs to talk?

Do we really need to attend another Bible study? The authors of this book are die-hard supporters of scriptural learning, but sometimes our church schedules are overactive, overbooked, or overprogrammed. And we know of one pastor who asked provocatively, "What is the point in educating ourselves about the gospel above and beyond our willingness to obey it?" Here's another question, more playful but no less serious: What would happen if we started spending so much time with the unbelievers or the unchurched people we know that we didn't have the time to finish reading this book? Or is it more likely that an unchurched or unbelieving person would reach out to us and we'd say, "Sorry, I don't have time to spend with you. I have to finish reading this book about relational evangelism!"

Have our social circles shrunk to the point that we only relate to people who agree with us? It can be easier to hit it off with people who are a lot like us. And most of us do not have a surplus of close friends. So consciously or not, we will budget our relational energy, eager to maximize the return on our emotional investment. Why reach out to someone who has different core values, especially if those fundamental differences decrease the possibility that the relationship will be mutual and meaningful? There is good logic behind all of this, but it also severs opportunities for life sharing and faith sharing.

What would it take for you to make another friend? Attentiveness? Courage? Initiative? Prayer? Don't think for a moment that the Holy Spirit isn't pulling for us in this task. We are convinced that if we simply ask God to bring someone into our life who needs friendship, a spiritual home, or the gospel, God will come through and that person will appear.

Perhaps it's true that some of us, by vocation or living arrangement, are completely surrounded by other believers. If you absolutely cannot find a single unchurched or unbelieving person in your life (a premise we might question), redouble your efforts to show hospitality to the guests who visit your church. Notice these newcomers, and graciously excuse yourself from conversations with your church friends—they'll understand.

Greet your church's guests. Look them in the eye, invite them to coffee, and welcome them as Christ welcomed you.

"I'd like to share my faith, but I'm just too busy. There isn't enough time to do it."

We (Fred and Jeremy) are active people. We do not struggle with sloth, and we do not suffer from having an excess of free time. Further, we appreciate that there are overstuffed seasons of life. But all of us should consider our relationship with busyness.

Busyness can be used as an excuse for anything. We've heard six-year-olds tell their grandparents that they are too busy to come over and play (they were watching cartoons). We've heard the same from teens who spend hours everyday playing video games. To claim that we are victims of the clock has become an all-purpose, culturally acceptable trump card.

Busyness can be the sign of an activity addiction, poor priorities, or simply the need to manage our time more effectively. If our schedule is so tight that we have squeezed out any possibility for relationship, that may be an indication we are living unsustainably. If faith sharing is truly impossible for us, a rebalance of work and rest might be in order. In this case, "not enough time" could be a symptom and not the problem.

Busyness can also be a sign of healthy ambition and God-given competence. Some of the busiest people we know are also some of the most capable people we know. If this describes you, we're confident that you can find great evangelistic opportunities if you make time for it. Ask other busy people how they manage to share their life and faith. Eat lunch at a park by yourself, and ask the Lord what you should do. Ask for eyes to see others who need a touch of grace. Create simple systems to respond quickly with care for others. Keep greeting cards on hand, keep a florist on speed-dial, or text one person a day with an "I'm praying for you" message. But there is no replacement for *making time* for relationships, knowing that you'll receive in the giving.

"I'm okay with evangelism in theory, but I'm not sure I want to share my life with others. Deep down, I don't want other people to know me."

We know one church where a shockingly high percentage of those who belong have been estranged from their families. As pastors, we've had parishioners come to us privately and say, "I've been leading a double life." And we know more than a few disciples who feel their day-to-day life simply does not measure up to the teachings of Jesus.

In many ways, interpersonal distance creates a kind of safety. If no one ever sees our face, we'll never need to save face. But if we invite anyone into our life, we know that they are likely to see us, warts and all. Many of us are just not good at relationships. That's why we avoid them. And while self-isolation is common, it's not safe in the long run. We know one church-planting guru who constantly tells new church planters, "The most dangerous thing we can do is be alone." We need others, but it seems part of the human condition to avoid the things we need the most.

We suspect that Christians and non-Christians avoid relationships for the same reason: we fear being known. If this rings true for you, even a little, we implore you to do something about it. If you're aware that your life is genuinely askew, perhaps you need to go to your pastor. Confess if need be, and ask for his or her support and guidance. (Remember that a good pastor lives and breathes to help people grow in Christ and has probably heard worse.) If you can recognize that you strain every relationship you are a part of, get help, talk to someone you trust, and consider finding a counselor. If you are worried your life somehow doesn't measure up, we think you should still take the risk of inviting other imperfect people into your imperfect life in Jesus' name. Besides, the point isn't perfectionism; its proximity. Let the vulnerability of closeness grow your integrity, humility, and witness. And remember the angelic imperative: "Do not be afraid."

"I'm uncomfortable, and I don't want to be rejected. I'm afraid I'll look foolish."

If I buy a billboard emblazoned with a Christian message, I am free to call that evangelism if I wish. But the reality is that that media will probably not create committed disciples of Jesus. What it will do with great effectiveness is to ensure that I will never, ever face rejection. We don't advocate evangelism methods that are pushy or one-sided, but we do suspect that the overassertiveness, overconfidence, and overstatements do successfully serve a hidden purpose: they protect the heart of the evangelist.

Faith sharing is risky, and no amount of softeners or diplomacy will change that. Discomfort, rejection, and awkwardness are always realistic possibilities. Relational evangelism is especially risky. This is because the power and the danger of relational evangelism come from the same place. It is a *profoundly personalized* venture. Our hearts are on the line.

If it is truly our comfort that we wish to preserve, remember that we are committed to a Lord who was crucified on a cross and who invites us to take up our cross. Crucifixion is not a comfortable process. Yes, the Holy Spirit is the Comforter. And yes, we believe that comfort is an indispensible ministry of the church and of the Trinity. But comfort can also be spiritually fatal. It could be that our miniscule comfort zones serve as invisible barriers that protect us from the sacrificial adventure that the Holy Spirit is calling us to.

For more on this, see Chapter 8, "Embracing Risk."

"I don't want to admit it, but I'm afraid of growth. I like the church as it is right now, and I am not sure I want new people."

We rarely hear this confession so plainly spoken, in part because it is too self-implicating. But we suspect it is one of the major reasons we resist sharing our faith and inviting others to church. What we hear more often is superficial agreement to a growth goal but deep resistance to the steps it takes to reach that goal.

Growing a church is like shrinking a waistline. Imagine you're a physician and one of your patients said, "Doc, I'd like to lose weight."

"Good for you! Are you going to join a gym?"

"No."

"Work out on your own?"

"Never."

"Change your diet?"

"Absolutely not."

"Uh, can we talk more about this?"

"No way. I just want to lose weight!"

It wouldn't take long to lose patience with your patient. And church growth is a lot like weight loss. We like the idea, but we resist the lifestyle changes that are necessary to reach that goal. We know of one denominational leader who says sharply, "All churches say they want to grow, but most of them are liars."

We've heard a small minority of church members tell us, "We don't need new people." A doubtful assertion, but let's suppose for a moment that things at your church are hunky-dory. Let's assume that you have plenty of mature, committed disciples, plenty of money, clarity of vision, and are on an upward trajectory in every respect. Great! But super circumstances do not excuse us from the Great Commission. The call to make disciples is not situational. Jesus never said, "Booming churches, you're off the hook. But if your church is shrinking, hurry up and make disciples like crazy … until you've stabilized. Then go back to doing your own thing once you've avoided institutional disaster." This is the spiritual equivalent of a crash diet. We think that God is using the decline of our institutions to motivate us to share our faith and to call us to what we should have been doing all along.

In any area of our life, most of us are acutely aware of the cost of parting ways with beloved norms and leaving the safety of the familiar. So we need to come clean about the tremendous disincentives for pastors and other leaders to initiate change, and we need to say plainly that initiating a change is no guarantee of positive results. Like the recently freed Hebrews who pined for the stability of well-fed slavery, we often prefer dead certainty to what Walter Bruggemann calls "the threat of life." But to change or not to change, there is a price to be paid either way. Decline costs. So does growth. And God had given us a terrifying degree of latitude, not only to count to the cost but also to pay the price of our choosing.

"I guess I just have baggage with evangelism."

This is another confession that few people have the guts to name with frankness, but it's a widespread phenomenon. We began this book with the assumption that everybody has a bad evangelism story. And we continue with the assertion that such baggage does not earn us a pass. By all means, work to understand what went wrong. And by all means, forgive and move on.

The Silent Pentecost

Jimmy is a young lay leader at a large charismatic congregation in the Midwest, and he told us this story. "My church loves to worship. We stand up, we raise our hands, we sing, we dance, we shout, and we speak in tongues. We do it all, and we are very, very loud. But I know that the Spirit has *really* moved among us when I look up and realize every single person is moved to silence. It doesn't happen often. Silence might not seem like an outrageous move of the Spirit, but for us it is. I'm not saying that Christ isn't in us as we stand and shout, but for us, the high volume and big expressions come naturally and easily. God's power is most present when we have been moved beyond our natural tendencies."

This may be why reluctant evangelists are the best evangelists: it doesn't come naturally. When we abandon our armchair critiques and allow our concerns to inform our effort, we become principled practitioners rather than infallible abstainers. When we dig at the roots of our resistance, reluctance, and reticence, our discipleship becomes both more mature and more radical. And then perhaps God's Spirit can move us outrageously beyond our natural tendencies. God's power is revealed in our weakness.

Chapter 4

LEARNING HOSPITALITY

Abby was a retired schoolteacher living in the Midwest. Although she had serious misgivings about the "fire and brimstone" preachers on TV, she had no qualms with evangelism or church growth. She knew Christ was the bedrock of her life, she believed in the tangible love expressed by her home congregation, and she saw no reason to make a secret of such good things. It was also no secret that Abby saw the same aging faces in worship week after week. She was justifiably worried about the sustainability of the church that sustained her. So for all the right reasons, Abby wanted to reach out.

One Sunday, a single young woman appeared in worship. No one knew who invited her or where she was from. Abby tried to hide her exhilaration. A real-live visitor! But Abby's excitement shifted uncomfortably when she saw the members of her church, people she knew to be loving and Christlike, only staring awkwardly at their guest. *Why aren't they talking with her? She seems so nice!* Abby thought, her anxiety rising. Abby didn't hear a word of the liturgy; she was too preoccupied with how poorly her friends were responding to this fast-closing window of opportunity.

By the end of the benediction, Abby's heart was flooded with a potent mix of thrill and panic. She was determined to take matters into her own hands. No one had greeted this lovely young woman, so she had to act fast! Abby rushed across the sanctuary, and when the young woman turned to face her, Abby surprised herself by grabbing the face of the young woman with both hands and exclaiming, "Oh, thank God. Thank God! We need young people!"

Hospitality: we're not as good as we think we are. Even if we are not prone to social gaffs, even if we are educated people, even if we are seasoned saints, and even if we say we know better. The true story of Abby is Exhibit A. And we cannot assume that others know how to show Christian hospitality. Like every other aspect of our discipleship, hospitality needs to be taught, modeled, reminded, and encouraged.

Hospitality in the Bible: Nowhere and Everywhere

Some biblical topics are clearly defined or explained. If you want to know what love is, turn to the parts of the Bible that begin with "Love is …" (1 Corinthians 13 and 1 John 4:10 come to mind). With other biblical topics, the *concept* is present even if the *word* is not. Isaiah 6 is considered a foundational text on the subject of Christian worship, but the term *worship* is nowhere to be found. The book of Esther never mentions the word *God*. But God's power, sovereignty, and providence are conspicuous throughout. In the Gospels, the resurrection of Jesus is definite, but it is not defined; it is witnessed and proclaimed, but not explained. Biblical hospitality is much the same way. There is no strict definition for biblical hospitality, no part of the Bible that begins with "Hospitality is …" Throughout the Bible, hospitality is less likely to be named and more likely to be demonstrated, narrated, embodied, or commanded. In fact, as a concept, hospitality permeates Scripture. Consider:

Hospitality and Eden. The garden of Paradise was God's ultimate provision for Adam and Eve where more than they

47

could need, ask for, or imagine was made ready for them before they arrived. Eden was the gift of God's abiding presence and holy hospitality.

Hospitality and Abraham. In Genesis 18, Abraham's hospitality is on display in great detail as he notices, greets, honors, shelters, and feeds three strangers. A generous welcome becomes a divine encounter where Abraham hears of God's promise, judgment, and nearness. By opening his life to the stranger, God changed the course of Abraham's life forever.

Hospitality and the Law. It should come as no surprise that a people who knew slavery and landlessness also had laws like Leviticus 19:34: "The alien who resides with you shall be to you as the citizen among you; you shall love the alien as yourself, for you were aliens in the land of Egypt: I am the LORD your God." Others like it can be found.

Hospitality and Wisdom Literature. Some words are intuitive, such as "Better is a dry morsel with quiet than a house full of feasting with strife" (Proverbs 17:1), others are counterintuitive like "If your enemies are hungry, give them bread to eat; and if they are thirsty, give them water to drink" (Proverbs 25:21), but all reveal a God with hospitality in mind, who prepares "a table before me in the presence of my enemies" (Psalm 23:5).

Hospitality and the Prophets. In 1 Kings 17, a hopeless, impoverished single mother welcomes an unknown man into her home to share her last meal. A risky move. But the results were impossibly good—bottomless nourishment, her son's resurrection, and hope restored. Opening her humble door and her paltry pantry to the unfamiliar person eventually meant opening her life to the true word of the Lord.

Hospitality and the birth of Jesus. I'll never forget the youth leader who said, "Jesus was born in a barn." It's funny, but the implications are serious. The inability or unwillingness of others to extend humane shelter to a traveling, pregnant woman speaks volumes. And we find in that story the indictment of our own unresponsive hearts and lukewarm reception to Jesus and the stranger.

Hospitality and the life of Jesus. The meals, teachings, healings, travel, foot washing, and anointing … how much of Jesus' ministry took place in people's homes? Hospitality can turn a residence into a sanctuary. But Jesus' spirit of hospitality transcended buildings and real estate. He welcomed children, dined with tax collectors, and touched the diseased. In a religious context that focused on holy places (like the Jerusalem temple and the Promised Land generally), Jesus demonstrated God's open-air kindness and portable peace with his go-anywhere hospitality.

Hospitality and the crucifixion of Jesus. The cross was about hostility, the opposite of hospitality in every respect. It was a spectacle of violence, shame, and rejection. And yet, radically redeemed and reversed by Christ, the cross becomes the very symbol of life and God's hospitality, where crucifiers are forgiven and the wounds of Jesus heal (1 Peter 2:24).

Hospitality and the church. The first-century discipleship movement gathered in residences, organized meals for widows, and read the epistles aloud in their home churches. Undeniably, Christian hospitality was part of the very fabric of the resurrection community.

Hospitality and heaven. The kingdom of heaven is God's ultimate provision, where more than we could need, ask for, or imagine is made ready for us before we arrive. It is the gift of God's abiding presence and holy hospitality.

If you did a word search for *hospitality* in the Bible, you'd only find a few references. But if you grabbed a pair of scissors and cut all the *demonstrations* of hospitality out of the Bible, you'd start with a holy book and end up with a book full of holes.

Biblical hospitality is different than the hospitality industry, and it's different than American Southern hospitality. Biblical hospitality is not about luxury, entertainment, or impressing people. It's not about fancy houses. It's not just for women, and it's not just for partygoers and party-throwers. It's far, far beyond etiquette or friendliness. Biblical hospitality is the interpersonal expression of a theological truth: we welcome others as Christ has welcomed us.

In the New Testament, the Greek word translated as "hospitality" is *philoxenia*. It's essentially a two-part word. The first part, *philo*, means "love." The second part, *xenia*, means "stranger." (Think of it as the opposite of xenophobia, which is the hatred or fear of strangers.) We're familiar with the phrase "To know them is to love them." But biblical hospitality is literally "stranger love," and few of us have made the effort to love someone *before* we know them.

Henri Nouwen was a Roman Catholic priest who left Ivy League teaching positions to serve and care for developmentally disabled people. In his book *Reaching Out: The Three Movements of the Spiritual Life*, he writes, "Hospitality means primarily the creation of free space where the stranger can enter and become a friend instead of an enemy. Hospitality is not to change people, but to offer them space where change can take place."

Fred Bernhard is not as famous as Henri Nouwen, but he's a nice guy, and we think that should count for something. Fred has also devoted his academic and pastoral life to the practice of Christian hospitality, which he defines as "The attitude and practice of providing the atmosphere and opportunities, however risky, in which strangers are free to become friends, thereby feeling accepted, included, and loved. The relationship thus opens up the possibility for eventual communion among the host, the stranger, and God."

But the lack of an explicit definition for hospitality in the Bible itself is worthy of reflection. Why are definitions scarce while examples abound? Perhaps the ability to *define* something is not as important as the ability to *do* it.

Less Like Martha Stewart, More Like Mary Magdalene: Hospitality and Your Church

Obviously, the practice of Christian hospitality goes far beyond what happens on your church's property. But how we treat people always sends a spiritual message. Don't tell your pastor, but an uncommonly warm welcome is probably more important than the sermon! We don't have to be a diva hostess or an anxious entertainer; we just have to view our hospitable efforts as ultimately directed toward Jesus. Here's a partial list of practical suggestions on making your church more hospitable.

Do a Hospitality Audit

Some time ago, we met with a church consultant in his home congregation. When we pulled into the quiet parking lot, we were mildly alarmed by multiple signs threatening to tow unauthorized vehicles. Since this consultant made his living in part by assessing churches and advising them to remove such signage, we wondered what extreme circumstances necessitated this exception. When we asked him if our cars were safely parked, he looked puzzled. Then we pointed out the signs. His eyes registered a flash of realization, and he dropped his shoulders, sighing, "Oh no. I've been here too long. I've seen those signs so many times I don't even notice them anymore."

We later found that the signs had been erected twenty years earlier. At that time, there were a few teens from the neighborhood who found the church parking lot to be irresistibly romantic. The reference to a tow company was a bluff intended to scare the young people who would park in the church lot and steam up their car windows. Of course, the teens ignored the signs, so the bluff never worked. But for two decades and three pastors, the signs were taken seriously by first-time visitors who wondered if their automobiles might be hauled away.

Walk around your property and ask yourself the following:

- Is the parking and front door clearly designated? Are restrooms, classrooms, and other areas obviously apparent to someone who has never been in that building before? Remember that clear signage is not a replacement for smiling and informative human beings. And human beings are not a replacement for clear signage.
- Is the landscaping well kept? It's doesn't have to say, "Opulence," but it shouldn't say, "Water me."
- Does the entrance feel like home? Or does clutter reign in a dimly lit foyer?
- Are children's areas clean, well stocked, accessible, and safe? Do those who teach or provide childcare inspire confidence in parents who meet them for the first time? Do those who greet adult guests also enthusiastically acknowledge their children and make them part of the conversation where possible?
- Do ramps, elevators, and lift chairs that are intended to serve those with special needs actually work? And is there an easily accessible human being in your church who knows how they work?
- Are there quirks to your worship space that need to be minimized, or beautiful character traits that could be maximized?

We know of one church in the Southeast that was embarrassed when we pointed out the glaringly obvious mildew stains on the bathroom doors. (At least the stains were obvious to us. Longtime members had been ignoring them for a decade at least.) After ferociously scrubbing away the fungi, one committee member came to us and said, "There! Now people from the neighborhood ought to start coming."

We learned two things from this exchange. First, we are often blind to our own inhospitality. The same people who tolerated uncleanliness in the church restroom would never have allowed the same thing in their homes (yes, we visited their homes). And the absurd equation "clean bathrooms = visitors" was not expressed by an unintelligent person but by a committed Christian and white-collar professional. Had this person *read* these words on the printed page, rather than having spoken them into thin air, they would respond with the same incredulity you and I did just now. Second, removing barriers is not the same as generating capacity. Dirty bathrooms can be enough to repulse people, but clean bathrooms are not enough to attract people.

This might be the limitation of the hospitality audit: it can help you clear the way, but it won't guarantee anybody will walk the path. Hospitality will touch the lives of those who come into our sphere of influence, but it won't always bring people into our sphere of influence. This is why we also need to focus on making friends (Chapter 5), inviting people (Chapter 6), and finding words (Chapter 7).

Train, Train, Train … Repeat

Theologically speaking, the church is the living, mystical, soul-changing, universal body of Christ. But tangibly speaking, churches are volunteer organizations, and overworked organizers are often relieved just to have willing souls and warm bodies. We've been there, so we understand. But hospitality requires more than a warm body. Just because a person is willing does not mean he or she is able, and a believer can have sterling character and still lack the spiritual gifts or the practical know-how no matter the task.

In one sense, we are made into the church by the saving power and eternal love of Christ. First Corinthians 12:27 is a declaration: "*You are* the body of Christ" (emphasis added). Through Christ, the church is what we are. In another sense, we have to be taught how to be the church. The whole of 1 Corinthians 12 reveals that the body does not always know how to be the body. Training in hospitality can be one way to close the gap between our theological identity and our tangible interactions.

When you train folks in your faith community, consider giving specific instructions that are, in the words of one business leader, "Sesame Street simple." How should we respond to guests who visit our worship services? Walk across the room. Smile. Look them in the eye. Shake hands. Tell them your name. Ask them what their name is. Breathe. Relax. Remember that if this is your home church, guests are on your turf, and they are the ones taking the risk by entering a room full of strangers. Say, "We're glad you're here." Give one sincere compliment. Ask, "What brings you here?" Listen carefully. Introduce them to someone else in your church. Hold the door open. Guileless simplicity works wonders. And an eight-year-old can do this.

(For more on greeter training, we recommend *The First 30 Seconds: A Guide to Hospitality for Greeters and Ushers*, by S. Joan Hershey. See <ins>http://www.e3ministrygroup.com/</ins>)

Notice Newcomers

We know of one small church that decried the total lack of first-time guests in their worship services. "We keep praying for our church to grow, and it doesn't!" they said despairingly. But when we looked at their guest registry ("We have a guest registry?"), we found evidence of about thirty first-time visitors in the last year. This of course didn't include the people who didn't bother to record their presence in the unmanned registry. Do the math. This church was successfully ignoring at least one guest every other week. Why? Because longtime members were busy having conversations with longtime friends, others were occupied with committee business before and after worship, and we suspected that a few (including the pastor) were willfully oblivious. The sad fact is that they were too distracted to realize their prayers were being answered. Pay attention!

Cultivate Culture and Systems

By "culture" we mean the hard-to-define collection of attributes, attitudes, norms, and patterns of a community. Your church's culture might not be written down, but it's detectable. We've heard people talk about churches having a "vibe," a "tone," or an "organic identity," which sounds touchy-feely and New Age-y until you're in the room and sense the chemistry for yourself.

By "systems" we mean the intentional, formal, organizational plans for making your community of faith happen. This often looks like boards, committees, action groups, responsibilities, teams, bylaws, and official positions of impact and influence.

Our point is that they both matter. Culture is no replacement for systems, and systems are no replacement for culture.

A first-time guest at our church recently told me, "I have never been to a church that is so welcoming. Most churches have greeters, but they hand you the bulletin and say, 'Good morning,' and that's about it. I can go to Walmart and get a greeting like that. But when I came to this congregation, people who were not official greeters greeted me. People who clearly had no position went out of their way to seek me out. It's unexpected and infectious." This affirmation demonstrates a sharp perceptivity. What this person was able to detect was not just the systems (formal greeters) but also the culture (the spirit of welcome) in the churches they visited.

Take the initiative to develop and sustain a culture of hospitality. If you're a leader of any kind in your church, reinforce with gentle relentlessness the sort of actions and attitudes you want to see. If you preach, tell true stories in your sermons about times when you saw hospitality in action—or hospitality *inaction*. Continually make the connection between what we believe and how we treat those around us. When it comes to welcoming newcomers at your church, if you see your fellow church members come on too strong (or not strong enough), it behooves the leadership to give guidance quickly, kindly, and directly. Note and encourage people who go out of their way to do little things for others and celebrate those micro-initiatives for the spiritual victories that they are. Climate warms one degree at a time, and communal sincerity is undeniable.

But it's hard to give a wholehearted welcome when you're winging it, so organize your efforts. Ensure support, and be diligent. Make sure you can count on your volunteers, and make sure your volunteers can count on you. Expect guests and plan for them. Some churches, in addition to greeters, have a designated "nice guy/gal" or "Invisible Greeter" whose job is to simply walk around the church building and grounds and notice those whom others seem to miss. Plan to go the extra mile! Recruit umbrella-wielding volunteers who will rush out to the parking lot and offer to escort people inside when the weather is bad. While there is a limit to which we can systematize hospitality, we can unintentionally systematize carelessness by sloppy or nonexistent systems.

Watch Your Language: Visitor Kryptonite

Here are just a few things you can say if you want to make guests feel foolish, uncomfortable, unwelcome, or insulted:

- "Where is your husband?" (Spoken to a single woman)
- "So who are you related to in this church?"
- "Nice outfit." (Spoken with sarcasm. Remarkably, we've heard this several times.)
- "We're all familiar with the biblical story of ..." (Spoken by preachers and teachers)
- "Can you tell your children to be quiet/stop running?" (Spoken to a parent. Dirty looks can express the same sentiment.)

- "If you're visiting our church today, please stand up!" (Spoken by a pastor or worship leader during the service.)
- Crude sexual references are completely out of bounds. You'd think we wouldn't have to say this, but our experience has shown us that we do.

Some denominations are largely comprised of immigrant groups, and for people in the know, certain last names are common. I (Jeremy) am a Church of the Brethren pastor but have been told more than once by longtime Anabaptists, "Ashworth!? That's not a Brethren name!" Without fail, my inadequate familial pedigree was pointed out within the first three minutes of the conversation (yes, I have begun to check my watch in these situations). Other names are well-known in a particular community, either as famous or infamous local dynasties. "Oh, you're a part of *that* family." And other names may simply be unfamiliar to us culturally or ethnically. We once heard a white woman, who seemed unable to comprehend the African-American name Uwaanza, stammering, "What kind of a name is *that*?" At one church I served, our afterschool program involved three Burmese boys, all named Pi (pronounced "pee"). Sound strange? Well, white guys like me just need to get used to it. The Bible is crammed full of names that aren't from our culture either.

This isn't just about tolerance or familiarity. Many of our actions are a subtle shibboleth that informally but powerfully delineates the insider and the outsider (see Judges 12:5–6). Resist the urge to do an impromptu genealogical background check before extending a full welcome to someone, and remember that the basis of our welcome is Jesus, "the name that is above every name" (Philippians 2:9).

Get Changed

Hospitality changes everybody. And even though it seems innocuous, a hospitable experience on Sunday mornings has the potential to seep into our whole lives.

The way we talk about and practice many of our spiritual disciplines can cause our faith to be unintentionally compartmentalized. In my congregation, we gather for one weekly sixty-minute span of time that we call "worship." Most churches do. But despite the title of this gathering, worship in its truest sense is infinitely deeper than this single, hour-long event. Worship is the Christian lifestyle. For most of my life, I have understood prayer as the verbiage inserted between the opening words *Dear God* and the closing word *Amen*. But prayer at its widest is not bracketed. It is the ongoing conversation with God, a continual communion with the Holy Spirit, as constant as breath and as uncontained as the wind. Baptism is our public declaration of the deadness of sin and our unashamed immersion into the life of the Trinity. But baptism is not somehow over when we wipe off the water. The reality does not evaporate when the ritual concludes.

At worst, our spiritual disciplines are isolated incidents of piety. But at best, our spiritual disciplines are the beginning of a new way of life in Christ Jesus. It is during that hour on Sunday mornings that we remind ourselves that worship is not just an hour on Sunday mornings. It is through my stop-and-start prayers that I have learned to pray without ceasing. Even the songs I sing in church extend beyond the final stanza. When my vocal chords have ceased vibrating, there is still a reverberation in my heart and an echo in my soul that I will sometimes carry all week long.

So what does this have to do with hospitality and your church?

We want your church to be friendly. But if your church is *just* friendly, well, we're not sure that matters much. Jesus didn't die on a cross and come back from the dead to teach us social skills. If Christian hospitality is a code of conduct restricted to an hour a week, we are setting ourselves up to be hypocrites. It does no good to be nice on Sunday and mean on Monday. And if efforts like this are seen as just another program for your church, it probably won't accomplish much either. Some churches have jumped on so many short-term bandwagons they now suffer from what we call "program fatigue."

Although it may begin as a Sunday-morning effort, biblical hospitality can and should gradually become a way of life. Noticing newcomers will actually help you love others. Sound like a stretch? It isn't. How can we love others if we don't even notice them? How we treat others always sends a spiritual message. This is true not only for those who step foot on our church's real estate but also for those who enter our other spheres of influence: our work zones, play areas, or any other places we frequent in our weekly routines. Noticing people in church can help us begin to notice people everywhere.

Ephesians 4:27 tells us to not give the Devil a foothold. We know of no better way to do this than to give the Holy Spirit a foothold, to provide a scant opening and secure position in our lives from which further progress can be made. Mountains are taken one foothold at a time. We have friends who view Sunday worship as a waste of the morning. Their vision is too small. Our hope for Sunday worship is not just to waste the morning but also to ruin the whole week. Even more, it should contain the potential to, as one pastor put it, "Let Jesus ruin your life!" Any spiritual discipline, be it Sunday worship, personal prayer, singing together, or showing hospitality, is in fact a holy toehold. The point is to provide a sacred opportunity, to aid and abet the Holy Spirit to be an accomplice and an accessory for God's kingdom that is invading both our life and our world. What begins as one person welcoming another person is actually the beginning of an invitation to ongoing, non-compartmentalized discipleship for everyone involved. When this happens, both our churches and our lives can be, in the words of Bill Easum, "A safe place to hear a dangerous gospel, not a dangerous place to hear a safe gospel." [2]

---

[2]   Bill Easum is a Texas-based author and church consultant, and we heard him share this line at a recent seminar.

Chapter 5

MAKING FRIENDS

There's people been friendly
But they'd never be your friend
Sometimes this has bent me to the ground
—"Elijah" from the album *Rich Mullins*

Missing Pieces

I was a nerd in college. Of course, I was a nerd before then, and I'm still kind of nerdy, although these days I call myself a "church nerd" and try to make a living from it. But then I was definitely a nerd, and among the many socially impaired aspects of my collegiate geekdom was a passion for complicated board games. Not only did I enjoy playing them, I also relished researching, collecting, and obsessively curating their hundreds of parts and pieces. I pursued this absorbing pastime while living with other mild-mannered ministry students in a large, quiet, out-of-the-way campus house. My housemates and I had plenty in common, but in general they were more athletic and hygienic and had better social skills than me.

One day, a new student at the college heard me whining about how I was missing pieces from one of my games. He was a nerd too, but he was one of the shy and introverted varieties, the kind that does not bleat vociferously when life interferes with eccentric hobbies. I didn't even notice I had been complaining, but he certainly did, and one evening he appeared on the front step of our house. He shuffled his feet, asked for me, and when I came to the door, he thrust a plastic baggie of game pieces in my direction. "Here, this will help," he said, almost inaudibly. With barely a flash of eye contact, he turned and scurried into the night. I examined the bag's contents closely. The pieces he gave me could work in a pinch perhaps, but they were from a different game, and not what I was looking for. Bummer.

When I pointed this out to my housemates lounging in the living room, they sat bolt upright, incredulous at my ingratitude. "Jeremy, he came all the way over here to give you a *gift*! Don't you see what's really going on here? *He wants to be your friend.*" While all I could see was an incomplete collection, the guys who lived with me saw relational initiative, a gesture of fledgling friendship. I stood in the living room, blinking.

Maybe that's what happens when our world shrinks to the size of our own interests. Or maybe some of us are just not that good at relationships.

An Epidemic of Friendlessness

Nerds or not, it's our premise that most of us are not as good at relationships we'd like to think we are. If that sounds outrageous or insulting, consider how it is possible that so many therapists, advice columnists, and relationship gurus are kept in business. And speaking of business, it's also worth pointing out that not only are our lives brimming with countless superficial relationships, there is also the tendency for fake friendships to be leveraged as marketing tools. Our concept of connection has been cheapened and commoditized. I know lonely people who buy decorator items cheerily emblazoned with the word *community*. These tchotchkes are made by people they don't know and sold to them by people they don't know, but they purchase them because they somehow touch an ache of the heart.

We're not just advocating better social skills (although some of us need them). What concerns us is a subtly dangerous level of isolation, friendlessness, and seclusion. Being a likable loser may be awkward, but it's mostly harmless. We know too many who try for too long to get by with too few caring companions. And when a person realizes they have starved themselves socially, they scramble to microwave intimacy. It doesn't work.

Loneliness is a quiet scourge. While many human behaviors can be tracked, loneliness itself is hard to quantify. For example, we can chart the number of people who are taking antidepressants. CBS news reports that about 10 percent of people over the age of twelve are being medicated for depression. According to a US government study, suicide rates surged 30 percent in the last year among middle-class whites. We have one friend who served as a pastor in a region known for a 75-percent divorce rate, with Christians just as likely to divorce as non-Christians. In these and other situations, it's impossible to precisely weigh the invisible heft of loneliness. But as pastors, we (Fred and Jeremy) are convinced of the role played by isolation. Yes, the love of money is the root of all kinds of evil (1 Timothy 6:10). But social seclusion is fertile soil for sin and self-destruction.

Despite the proliferation of pseudo-friendships, most of us are still desperately hungry for the real thing, for connections that truly have meaning, and for people we can count on. If we are indeed experiencing an epidemic of loneliness, the good news is that the Good News has never been more timely, and a relational approach to sharing our faith can touch lives at their very point of need.

Insiders and Outsiders

When it comes to churchy insiders (like us) beginning to form friendships with those outside the church, there are two points worth remembering. First, those outside the church do not always view the church as a good thing, and often for good reason. Second, those outside the church are not always unbelievers.

Let's take the second point first. Many books about evangelism and faith sharing seem based on the assumption that unchurched people are all hardcore unbelievers. That assumption is just plain wrong. Worse, it can lead to approaches that are disrespectful, offensive, or at least not a good way to kick off a friendship. What we'd like to suggest is, like it or not, the categories of "churched" and "unchurched" are both fluid and nuanced. The catchall category "unchurched" describes people who are:

- *Ground Zero unbelievers.* These are people with absolutely no church background or Christian framework whatsoever. As pastors, it has been a privilege for us to shepherd people who, when we first met them, literally did not know what a hymn or a sermon was.
- *Bits-and-pieces unbelievers.* These folks are uninformed about Christianity and/or the church and thus make faith-related decisions based on whatever piecemeal experiences they have had.
- *Seriously burned unbelievers.* They have been betrayed, let down, hurt, or harmed by self-professed Christians whose anti-witness was more powerful than their witness.
- *Conveniently "burned" unbelievers.* They claim to be burned by Christians or by the church but actually have no intention of giving faith a fair shake. While some churches can absolutely be hurtful and hypocritical, some people will say they've been "hurt by the church" in order to garner sympathy. Others say they are "turned off by all the hypocrites," but use this as a socially acceptable excuse to never do what they never wanted to do in the first place.

- *"Why church?" unbelievers.* They do not think of themselves as having a problem with Christianity. They just don't see the benefit of church involvement.
- *Cautious seekers.* Are spiritually interested but socially cautious people who would probably check out our churches if they thought they would be welcomed.
- *Free-range believers.* Are believers who have come to Christ apart from the church and do not currently have a church home. These can be people that the Holy Spirit has reached before the church has.
- *Conversion collectors.* Consider themselves believers and have collected a series of conversion experiences in a variety of congregations but have never managed to connect with any single one. I (Jeremy) once met a fifteen-year-old boy who had been "saved" six times by as many churches, and I know adults with similar stories.
- *Believers with baggage.* They are resistant to joining a church because they have issues with commitment, maturity, unforgiveness, or perfectionism. We have pastored (and attempted to pastor) people who were somehow unready for life in community.
- *Reform-hungry believers.* They are certainly disciples of Jesus but are so turned off and ticked off by their decidedly un-Christian encounters with the church that they are actively looking outside and hoping for something better. If they found it, they'd join it.
- *Burned-out believers.* These are often people who have served in leadership positions and have had to carry unreasonable burdens or suffered emotionally expensive hardships as a result of their participation. One pastor calls these people "the overchurched."

These eleven "types" of unchurched people barely scratch the surface.

The reality is that being unchurched does not absolutely designate an unbeliever any more than being churched absolutely designates a believer. And in some instances, unchurched people do not require a case for Christ; they need a case for the church. Of course, the fact that "churched" and "unchurched" are not necessarily hard categories is both good news and bad news. Some of the "churched" people in your congregation are one bad experience, one scandal, one offense (real or perceived), or one lost relationship away from being "unchurched." But some of the "unchurched" people in your community are one great experience, one solid witness, one caring invitation, or one warm friendship away from being "churched."

Mind the Gap

There certainly are militant atheists and anti-theists in the world, but few people describe themselves in those terms. Gallop, Pew Forum, and Barna offer the following statistics:

- 78 percent of people in the United States identify as Christians.
- 9 percent identify with different faiths.
- 13 percent claim no religious identity.
- 63 percent claim to be a member of a church or a synagogue.
- About 1 in 4 people say they are in church or synagogue on a typical weekend.
- As many as 95 percent of people in the United States say they pray several times in any given week.

These values are not the polar opposite of Christianity. While it is true that the percentage of people in North America who claim no religious identity has increased, the reality is that most persons believe in God and far more identify with the Christian faith than with any other belief system. Of course, just because someone checks a box marked "Christian" on a survey does not mean they are a follower of Jesus. We're not saying that evangelism and discipleship are easy tasks, but we are saying that this data cannot indicate a uniformly hostile environment for faith sharing. Between believers and unbelievers, the churched and the unchurched, there seems to be both a values gap and a values overlap.

Oddly enough, perhaps the strongest commonality between churched and unchurched people is that they often view each other in uninformed, inaccurate, and stereotypical terms. From the one side, churched believers can be perceived as some combination of uninteresting, institutional, old, rigid, too-traditional, or too-trendy conformists who only care about money, power, and bad music. And from the other side, unchurched people (be they believers or not) can be seen as some combination of low-commitment, spiritually disinterested, materialistic partygoers worthy of research but not relationship. At times, these stereotypes contain some truth, but they are predominantly cheap and conveniently self-serving, particularly because they allow both parties to retain the moral high ground. When the Promised Land is wherever you currently stand, dismissal becomes easy, and there is no need for spiritual movement toward God or others.

Those who claim that the church is too institutional are probably right, but such qualms are rarely invoked when it comes to their participation in other institutions (schools, shopping malls, employers, Internet service providers). And those of us within the church who have taken little initiative toward our unchurched friends and neighbors have a convenient excuse for when our churches decline—we can blame the larger culture for its supposed spiritual disinterest. All of this would be silly if it were not so tragic. But there is a powerful possibility for Christian discipleship hidden in this mutual misunderstanding. When Christians and non-Christians sit down and get to know each other better, great things can happen for everyone involved. Those who are not disciples of Jesus get a better picture of what living faith is actually like, and those who are disciples of Jesus will find their faith grows in the sharing of it. So we say to both insiders and outsiders, "Make friends, and update your stereotypes!" Perhaps the values gap between believers and nonbelievers may not prove to be as resilient as the social gap between the churched and the unchurched.

Intentionality, Not Calculation

Christians, make friends. And when we say "friends," we mean friends. Some zealous believers have formed strategic, inauthentic relationships with unbelievers as a way to get them to convert. This is just another marketing scheme at best and a form of covert exploitation at worst. And when it's exposed for what it is, things usually end badly. We heard of one Christian woman who began exercising with a non-Christian woman for the sole purpose of winning her to Christ. Eventually, the non-Christian workout partner began to sense that something was strangely lopsided in the relationship and asked point-blank, "Am I your *project*?" Friendship is not about closing a deal.

Still, deep connections don't happen by accident. Somebody has to throw the party, extend the hand, risk rejection, and do the labor that love requires. Of course, relational evangelism should be natural and organic, but it's never effortless. If thriving friendships grew wild, easy, and free, there would be more of them. If passivity bore fruit and evangelism could be accomplished by doing nothing, our churches would be in better shape.

We recently heard a pastor call for "friendship without calculation," and we agree. Of course, the fact that the qualifier "without calculation" is required ought to be a sign to us that we have a wacky, twisted, bait-and-switch view of relationships. In the same breath, we're also promoting "friendship with intentionality." It's not controlling, but it is responsive. It's reactive and proactive and generously Christlike and purpose-full without being agenda-driven. After all, that's how love ought to be, right?

Friendship and the Bible

Before we were born, God expected our relationships to be messy. And in God's providential genius, we can find ourselves equipped with preemptive scriptural guidance. The book of Proverbs is a relational goldmine, and if you do some digging, you'll find valuable truths about gossip, loyalty, encouragement, and counsel. Here are just three nuggets we like:

1. "A fool takes no pleasure in understanding, but only in expressing personal opinion" (Proverbs 18:2). Notice the word *pleasure* here. One way to make this Proverb actionable is to *enjoy* the task of understanding others and let them know you get a kick out of seeing their perspective.
2. "As iron sharpens iron, so one person sharpens another" (Proverbs 27:17). Some of us avoid deeper conversations with others as a way of avoiding conflict. Contact means that sparks may fly, but it's better to be forged and sharp than rusty and dull.
3. "Those with good sense are slow to anger, and it is their glory to overlook an offense" (Proverbs 19:11). In the book *The Sacredness of Questioning Everything*, David Dark writes incisively, "The feeling of offendedness is invigorating … it summons a sense of being in the right, a certain strength, a kind of power, an espresso shot of righteous indignation." It's true that outrage at injustice is completely justified and morally called for. Just read the

biblical prophets. It's also true that our being offended is not an infallible spiritual barometer, and that many people who see themselves as being akin to modern-day prophets can also be needlessly angry and alone.

Before the hit TV show *Game of Thrones*, there was the high-stakes royal friendship of David and Jonathan in 1 Samuel. The tie that binds these men has a lot to teach us, and we couldn't help but notice these two dynamics:

1. *Friends choose against self-interest.* Jonathan had to pick between becoming the king or remaining a friend, and he famously chose his ally over his crown. David's heroism often steals the spotlight, but it is Jonathan's selflessness that stands in stark contrast to our tendency toward hungry self-seeking ("What can I get?") in our connections with others.

2. *Friendships are covenants.* The Bible uses the word *covenant* to describe the soul-deep, life-and-death alliance between God and his people. But in 1 Samuel 18:3 and 23:18, the bond between David and Jonathan is described in covenantal terms. This is not a disposable friendship. It's a responsible relationship and costly commitment in the midst of multiple roles and competing claims for loyalty. And as a covenant, it echoes the very faithfulness of God.

Relationships in the Bible are a rich and inexhaustible vein, so get busy digging! The Old Testament book of Ruth contains the bond of Naomi and Ruth. The book of Job details the hard-times conversations between Job and his friends. The New Testament holds the unexpected neighborliness of the Samaritan (Luke 10:29–37), the importance of interpersonal reconciliation and restoration (Matthew 18), and the countless "one-anothering" verses throughout the New Testament—serving one another in love (Galatians 5:13), forgiving one another (Ephesians 4:32), and bearing with one another (Colossians 3:13). This is not abstract philosophizing; it is immediately livable theology. As we recently heard one local pastor say, "Our goal is to be neighbors and friends to our neighbors and friends."

Sixteen Sweet Friendship Tips

Scripture is eternally irreplaceable, but it's not enough to be able to regurgitate Bible verses about friendships. We heard one pastor express concern about what he called "the Bible commandos" in his congregation. These people knew the Bible, but they were also unnecessarily abrasive and difficult to know and love, theologically orthodox but relationally insufferable. Like anything else, scriptural knowledge and religious experience can be used as a way to keep others away.

Thankfully, God's provision in the body of Christ includes people who exude warmth in a way that seems almost supernatural. We all know someone who can change the temperature of the room just by the power of his or her presence, and we consider this an underrated form of spiritual giftedness and applied kindness. That's why we've sat at the feet of these sisters and brothers to learn from them. Here are sixteen tips they've shared with us:

1. **It might actually be okay to start with stereotypes.** We heard these words from a pastor doing amazing youth ministry in Belfast, Northern Ireland. "There are no blank slates. Stereotypes and prejudices are natural; they are part of how we learn. So it's okay to *begin* a relationship with an idea of the other person in your head, but don't stay there. Once you get to know someone deeply, you'll see that no one fits neatly and completely into any category."

2. **Acceptance does not mean approval.** Jeremy had a college professor who always turned heads with this advice.

Some Christians are wary of having buddies who possess wildly varying values. The unease seems rooted in the idea that friendship somehow equals endorsement, or that a relationship somehow necessitates a tacit moral approval. We understand this logic, but think of Jesus. He was a friend of sinners and was no less a Savior for being such. On an interpersonal level, we can fully accept and embrace people without signing off on everything they think and do. The key, we think, is to maintain both compassion and boundaries. One minister says of his church, "'All welcome' does not mean 'anything goes.'" At best, it is the context of an established relationship that makes it possible to have deeper conversations about differing values.

3. **Initiate and respond.** Be proactive. Make the first move. Extend the invitation. Write the letter. Put yourself out there. So many of us think about this but never actually do it. And when you do, make the meeting a race to the bottom. Be the first to listen, the first to take out the trash, the first to give up your spot for someone else. At the same time, be reactive. If you ignore, you'll close the door. Return phone calls, e-mails, text messages, cards, and notes. Be alert to the gestures of fledgling friendship that others cautiously extend. Of course, you don't have to be frantic or hyper-connected, but be reasonably responsive because responsiveness shows care.

4. **Play ball.** A good conversation is like playing catch. One throws the ball; the other throws it back. This may be why a one-sided conversation is called a "pitch." Take turns talking. Listen, share, ask, listen, repeat.

5. **Sincerity and simplicity.** Rather than smothering someone with language, pick a few words that say it as best you can. And don't say it if you don't mean it. If we are eager to win someone's approval, it can be tempting to gush, but flattery is an unstable foundation for friendship.

71

6. **Move from compliment to encouragement.** Earnest, direct compliments go a long way to breaking the ice, even if the topic seems superficial, e.g. "Great dress." But compliments are also an opportunity to move beyond small talk. Ask deeper questions about seemingly superficial things, and find little ways to lift up the other person. "Every time I see you, you always look like you have it together. I'm impressed. How do you do that as a working mother of toddlers?" What begins as a kind observation can actually lead into biblical one-anothering. "Encourage one another" (1 Thessalonians 5:11).

7. **Listen for hearts.** In the back-and-forth game of toss that is conversation, notice the tone and content of what people are throwing out there. Expect their heart to spill over into their words (Luke 6:45), even if only fleetingly. And when it happens, respect their vulnerability. When it seems appropriate, express gentle curiosity.

8. **Follow up on the news.** Another opportunity to go deeper than small talk. What news was shared in the conversation? A new job? A health problem? After your chat, make mental note, take it to the Lord in prayer, and ask the person about it the next time you see him or her. Or make it a point to follow up afterward with a text, card, note, or other message to congratulate, comfort, or let them know you're thinking of and praying for them. Open the door to continued connection and say, "If you ever want to talk, let me know."

9. **Refuse intimidation.** Be it expensive suits or extensive facial piercings, hot bluster or cold silence, social intimidation is ubiquitous, and its influence is enormous. And those who know its power will wield it like a weapon or wear it like armor. Notice this and respect it, but remember that as followers of Jesus, we will use and define power much differently. Steadfastly refuse to be unsettled

by someone's appearance or mannerisms. Christ has come, died, and risen for them. The least we "little Christs" can do is to look past these social armaments and fearlessly look others in the eye. To the degree that the Holy Spirit makes you able, relate to everyone with Christ's spirit of disarming, unthreatened, and undeterred love.

10. **Expect the walking wounded ...** Remember the words of Scottish author and theologian Ian Maclaren, "Be kind, for everyone you meet is fighting a hard battle." This is painfully true.

11. **... but notice "normal" people.** We know several congregations filled with caring Christians who are consistently responsive to conspicuously high-needs individuals. But the downside of such compassion and generosity is that we can ignore people whose brokenness is not so glaring. Further, the dark side of any charity is that it can be addictively gratifying to help a needy person. So don't just grease the squeaky wheel; note those who by all appearances seem ordinary, regular, or "just fine."

12. **Don't hide behind service projects.** Some of our friends doing great kingdom work in long-term overseas missions and radical community-based ministries in the United States recently told us, "Service can be a way of insulating ourselves from relationships. We're so occupied with preparing the food and building the house that we actually keep the people—the hungry and the homeless—at a safe distance." We (Fred and Jeremy) are tireless advocates of well-thought-out service projects, but we also want to keep our eyes wide open to its downside. Some activities can protect us from engaging the souls we think we are serving, and sometimes in the name of serving others, we are actually serving ourselves.

13. **Walk calmly through the war zone.** Whether it's a seemingly polite party or a supposedly reverent worship

gathering, we should remember that in almost any group setting there will be a chain reaction of invisible emotional explosions. If a pretty woman or handsome man walks into the room, both attraction and jealousy will ensue. If a seemingly confident person shows up, he or she will unintentionally terrify at least a few of those around him or her. If someone in a group has obvious needs, his or her presence can trigger in others feelings of contempt, pity, or both. If a woman or man appears to be accomplished in some way, all they have to do is simply exist and others will feel ashamed by their own perceived shortcomings. Bursts of attraction, jealousy, fear, contempt, pity, and shame can decimate any chance of friendship before it even begins. So be aware of these dynamics, but refuse to let them deter or determine your efforts at knowing and loving others.

14. **Engage the story.** Everyone has a story. Ask about it by picking up on whatever threads of narrative are provided you. "I love your old car. How long have you had it? Do you work on it yourself?" Or, "Great tattoos. What does this symbol mean to you? When did you get it done?" Vehicles and body art may seem materialistic or frivolous, but under the right circumstances, a car or a tattoo can actually be an invitation to connect. Don't miss this invitation, and don't dismiss something that might be part of someone's emotional and spiritual résumé. We've heard responses like "I started working on cars with my dad. It was the best way for me to spend time with him." Or, "I got this tattoo when I was having a very hard year. Since things have turned around a little, I'm thinking of getting some new ink right beside it." This isn't small talk; it's big talk. Whenever we engage a person's narrative, we are also seeking where God is and has been present in this person's life as "the author and finisher" of their story (Hebrews 12:2).

15. **The problem is the solution.** A pastor we know who works in church revitalization pointed this out to us. Don't avoid hardships, as they can be the perfect place to start walking and talking better values. We all know people who are:
    - always needy
    - jealous, controlling, or critical of others
    - struggling with "frenemies" (A frenemy is a simultaneous mash-up of friend and enemy; it can be enemies or rivals who act like your friends or a friend who sucks the life out of you.)
    - caught in addictive, enabling, or codependent family systems
    - consistently bringing drama into the lives of those around them
    - needing help with both boundaries and compassion

This is messy territory. It also holds the potential to be sacred space and holy ground if we engage it and don't avoid it. One brilliant friend wrote in her journal,

> I think so often, especially as a Christian, I am tempted to ignore the ugly things in myself that stir me up … I gloss over my pain, skirt by my grief, avoid my undesired feelings … Who wants to say, 'Here you go, Bitterness. Sit down next to me, and let me ponder why there is such a bad taste in my mouth.' I certainly don't … I am starting to see, however, that this resistance to embrace my weaknesses, my undesired self, is not making me any better … it just keeps me in the same place.

She concluded that her difficulties were and are "the very places God wants to meet me." A healthy relationship, all by itself, is a powerful Christian witness. And when we engage our painfully relevant relationship issues with the help of Christ and the Christian community, we are improving our witness and are on the move toward redemption.

16. **Be vulnerable.** Jesus emptied himself, humbled himself, and "became obedient to the point of death—even death on a cross" (Philippians 2:7–8). We don't get the resurrection without the crucifixion, and we don't get the crucifixion without vulnerability. The amazing thing about vulnerability is not only is it embedded into what Christians believe about Jesus but it is also a necessary ingredient for any deeply meaningful relationship. To be unhidden and personally affected, even to a small degree, is patently unsafe. It's also intrinsic to both friendship and discipleship. (For more on this, see Chapter 8, "Embracing Risk.")

Friendships and Your Church

A woman I'll call Sally told us this true story:

> As kids, we were always in church. My mom and dad were constantly talking about God and Jesus and the Bible, and I forever saw my parents as these holy, righteous people. But one day during the sermon, our pastor had us do this strange thing … at least I thought it was strange at the time. He passed out papers and pencils and asked everyone to write down the answer to the question "Why do I go to church?" We didn't hand in the papers; it was just for our own benefit. I snuck a look at my dad's paper, thinking he'd written something really spiritual, but do you know what my dad wrote? "I'm here because my friends are here."

This is no anomaly. We know of one study, conducted by Christian Community, that contrasted more highly involved church members (Group A) with less highly involved church members (Group B). Group A was characterized by their regular presence in worship, faithful financial contributions, and involvement in one or more work or study groups in the church. Group B was characterized by their presence in worship only a couple of times a year, nominal financial contributions, and inconsistent involvement in any class or group. Here's how they responded to the following questions:

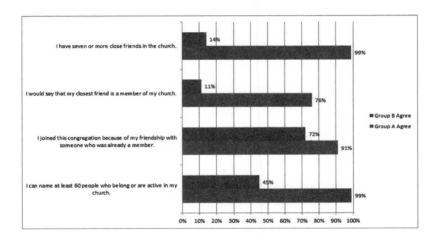

These contrasts are revealing. Friendship helps us get with a church, and it really helps us stay with a church. So the bottom line is, if we're not building friendships, we're not building our church.

Friendships, Your Pastor, and Relational Capacity

The pastor is not the church, but it matters how your pastor leads and serves. And if your church and your pastor are working at strengthening relationships in Jesus' name, it may help to calibrate our expectations by considering the following:

Know Thyself. We know of one experienced pastor who said that his visitation limit was thirty people per month. After decades of experience, he knew that if he was having in-depth conversations with less than seven or eight people per week, he was serving joyfully. More than that meant burnout. By contrast, we know a church planter who specializes in starting congregations from the ground up who says from experience that church planters can and should make contact with at least thirty unchurched people every day. Obviously these six-hundred-plus monthly contacts can't all be in-depth conversations, but a few of them are. The difference between this pastor and this church planter displays differing callings and capacities. It should also make the following very clear: our pastors cannot be the only people in the church who are reaching out by making friends. Declining churches often want a pastor who will "bring people in." But if the pastor is the primary (or only) person taking relational initiative, that makes for a slow, difficult turnaround at best and frustration and burnout at worst.

Where Everybody Doesn't Know Your Name. You might have two thousand Facebook friends, but the rule of thumb for real-life friends is closer to 150. That is, evolutionary psychology suggests that the maximum number of personal relationships that someone can sustain usually tops out at about 150 people. To us (Fred and Jeremy) this 1:150 ratio seems high. But we're not about to argue with evolutionary psychologists, especially since this seems to shed light on the fact that most American churches see less than 150 people in weekly worship attendance. Again, if the church's central relationship is with the one pastor (or with one or two well-known families or other leaders), the rule of 150 means the church probably won't get much bigger and its impact will be minimized.

Choose Wisely. Pastoral ministry can be strangely isolating. Part of it has to do with the fact that it's a lifestyle vocation and is rarely contained within a nine-to-five weekday rhythm. And part of it has to do with the fact that ministry requires the pastor to navigate multiple roles. If a plumber in my congregation comes over to fix my sink, to what degree am I his friend and/or his customer and/or his spiritual leader? A further wrinkle comes when well-meaning, lonely parishioners hope that the pastor (or the pastor's spouse) will be their default friend, their buddy on retainer. This complicated landscape might be why a Christian counselor we know says, "Most pastors are great as relational leaders, but they are lousy as real friends." At a minimum, the Elder Board, Church Board, Leadership Team, or Executive Committee needs to acknowledge the dangerous potential for relational fatigue on the part of their pastor. Even better would be to protect the right of the pastor and his or her family to make and maintain vital friendships both inside and outside the church. We know a lot of pastors who know a lot of people, but we've never met a pastor who complained of having too many real friends. (For more on this topic, check out the resource "Healthy Pastor, Healthy Church" available from E3 Ministry Group, see http:// e3ministrygroup.com/.)

An Unlikely Endorsement

There was a day when the local congregation ruled the social landscape. We know older people who, in their younger days, dated by attending church together. Why? "Because there was nothing else to do." Today that notion is hilariously quaint, as schedules are quickly saturated and social opportunities abound. Ladies' Aid groups have been replaced by knitting parties at the local coffeehouse. Meetup groups and local health clubs often relegate church gymnasiums to the sidelines. Perhaps karaoke is the new "hymn sing." However it happened, the church as dominant social hub has been dethroned.

A full house felt effortless when worship was the only show in town. But at its worst this was religion by default, and our churches became accustomed to easy critical mass. As this dynamic has waned and churches have declined, it has exposed a frustrated sense of entitlement: "We're here. Why don't they come anymore?" This is hardly an invitation to discipleship. Maybe the church never should have been on the throne in the first place.

In preparing to write this chapter, we did a lot of reading from several sources about how to make friends. We scoured websites, research papers, news articles, advice columns, and chatrooms, both religious and nonreligious. In all our research, we found one startling statement over and over: "If you want to make friends, start going to church."

Maybe it's because we're church nerds, but we found this fascinating. Secular mass media is not always faith-friendly, and the days of "nothing else to do" are long gone. But the bare fact is that *your church is being promoted by secular sources on the basis of its potential to help people make friends.* We're not saying that the unwashed masses will soon surge through your doors, but we are saying that when the *New York Times* recommends your church, to us that's pretty outrageous. And it leads us to ask, When the world meets your church, will they find friends?

> Your pain has changed me, your dream inspires
> Your face a memory, your hope a fire
> Your courage asks me what I'm afraid of
> and what I know of love
> —"I Saw What I Saw" from the album
> *Tell Me What You Know*

Chapter 6

EXTENDING INVITATIONS

Salsa and Sailing

Two of the best invitations I (Jeremy) ever received came shortly after my wife and I moved from Indiana to Seattle. At the time, we had lived our whole lives in small midwestern towns and didn't know a single soul in the Emerald City. The whole experience was brimming with anticipation and intimidation, the stuff of major life transitions.

We attended a new student gathering at my wife's school. I'd spent much of my time working with mainline congregations, which was to say that I was accustomed to Protestant architecture from the *Mad Men* era and was often the youngest person in the room by two or three decades. But this particular graduate school was housed in a former luggage factory (*The Christian Century* magazine called it "the hippest venue for a seminary ever"), and the student body was notably younger and funkier than I was (or am).

Following a creative and intense worship service, the students began socializing amidst the atmospheric backdrop of exposed brick and low lighting. My wife talked excitedly with new classmates. Temporarily adrift, I started walking. Slowly. I pretended I was cool, aloof, and not out of my league, trying hard to not try too hard. Ambling randomly, I soon found myself standing near a tall, gangly young man with an explosive mane of curly black hair.

I didn't know it at the time, but his name was Eratosthenes Fackenthall (easily the best name ever), nickname "Tos." What I did know was that this visual feast of a human being was recruiting salsa dancers. Although I don't recall his exact words, he was dramatically mid-sentence with arms upraised, saying something like "And we're going salsa dancing!" With manic exuberance, he motioned to the small, loose group of friends standing around him. "She's coming, and he's coming, and she's coming ..." At that moment, he spotted me, gawking at the spectacle of his exuberance. I was caught. "And you!" He pointed at me. "You should come too!" His wide hand opened. "Wanna come salsa dancing with us?" I felt a simultaneous rush of excitement and paralysis. I was terrified. I was in. It was that easy.

A day or so later, a guy named Ken invited me to go sailing. Like Tos, Ken is also tall and has curly hair. But unlike Tos, Ken is a pastor. So while Tos looks like a gloriously Greek Michael Bolton, Ken's hair is trimmed to a length appropriate for a religious professional who occasionally needs to appear soothing and approachable. Curly Ken asked me to go sailing with him at the historic Center for Wooden Boats in Seattle. He didn't know me, and I didn't know sailing, but sail we did. The sun was beaming, the wind was high, and I somehow got dumped in the water (my fault, not Ken's). He and I are friends to this day.

I lacked the courage to go salsa dancing with Tos and his posse, but I never forgot the indiscriminate welcome he unwittingly bestowed. I returned the favor by calling Tos on a rainy day and inviting him to see a depressing, artsy, independent movie I knew my wife would hate.

I'm smiling. Why did those invitations mean so much to me then? Why do they mean so much to me now? How are they so inexplicably good? It is as if something came alive in me just because I was invited.

The Upside-Down Invitation

Most people we know think of invitations as having a primary purpose and a secondary effect.

The primary purpose of an invitation is to inform people of an event or occasion. This is little more than data-sharing. And this information transfer is done for the purpose of requesting the presence and soliciting the participation of others so that the invited will hopefully choose to move from point A to point B at the right time.

"Come to our daughter's wedding this weekend!"

"You're invited to our son's graduation at the school tomorrow!"

"Your presence is requested at the camp meeting where we'll remove the warts from small furry animals!" (This is an actual invitation Jeremy once received.)

The secondary effect of an invitation is less concrete. At their very best, invitations make us feel some combination of being welcomed, involved, included, noticed, appreciated, valued, cared for, and thought of. More than hard data about time and place, there is a detectable but intangible benefit. Personal invitations can help us feel like we are not alone in the world, and if you think about it, that's a simple solution to a complex problem. Adding to the wonder is that invitations often achieve this warming, welcoming effect even if we are unable to attend the event itself. Perhaps we haven't moved from point A to point B by one inch, but something in the invitation itself has captured a fraction of our heart. In some small way, they can say we are loved.

Invitations seem to have a primary purpose and a secondary effect, but Christians are upside-down kingdom people, so it behooves us to ask the question in reverse. What if we have it backward? What if "getting people there" was secondary to engaging people, extending welcome, giving notice, and showing others that they are appreciated, cared for, and thought of? What if the secondary effect is actually the primary purpose?

On one level, this can sound absurd, even manipulative. Is this just feel-good theology and sanctified niceness? Selling an invisible product? Are we just invoking abstractions? We'll admit that it's easy to dismiss the invisible. But people of God have a name for something that is *substantial* even though it's *invisible*. That something is usually called *spiritual*.

What if invitation was not primarily a logistical act but primarily a spiritual act?

The Discipline of Invitation

Prayer, Bible reading, and worship are all spiritual disciplines. Richard Foster, champion for the spiritual disciplines, says in his classic book *The Celebration of Discipline*, "God has given us the Disciplines of the spiritual life as a means of receiving His grace. The Disciplines allow us to place ourselves before God so that He can transform us." While we couldn't find any single, comprehensive list of disciplines, they certainly include fasting, confession, service, journaling, singing, silence, and seeking spiritual direction. More than a laundry list of pious busywork, the disciplines are a possible means to an impossible end. Philosopher and professor Dallas Willard says in his book *The Spirit of the Disciplines,* "A discipline is any activity within our power that we engage in to enable us to do what we cannot do by direct effort." If we are going to have a relationship with God, the disciplines are indispensable.

In just about every case we can think of, the disciplines have both a tangible side and an intangible side. The tangible side is the part we humans actually do: read Scripture, speak prayer, or scribble lines in our journal. But prayer is more than talking, and journaling is more than ink on paper. There is an intangible, spiritual, or even a divine accomplishment that takes place. We are changed. Others change. Situations change. We know by faith that beyond our actions, God acts. In the disciplines, we experience a mysterious mingling of our action and God's power.

What if invitation, in its various forms, could also be a means of God's grace? What if invitation was a way to imitate Jesus, follow his commandments, and grow into his likeness? What if the intangible accomplishment of invitation was not simply the fringe benefit of niceness but the spiritual point? What if invitation was a way of showing love? If so, we think invitation could be added to the list of spiritual disciplines.

The RSVP Bible: An Invitation to Invitation

It should come as no surprise that the Bible is brimming with invitations. Isaiah 55:10–11 says,

> For as the rain and the snow come down from heaven, and do not return there until they have watered the earth, making it bring forth and sprout, giving seed to the sower and bread to the eater, so shall my word be that goes out from my mouth; *it shall not return to me empty, but it shall accomplish that which I purpose, and succeed in the thing for which I sent it.* (Emphasis added)

Various theologies of varying quality have grown from those verses. But at issue is the unthwarted effectiveness of God's Word as vital and reliable as the water cycle.

But what kind of word did God send? What kind of task is God trying to accomplish? In the immediate context, it sounds a lot like an invitation. And not just a single invitation but rather a host of them.

- There is an *invitation to abundance* and enjoyment. "Ho, everyone who thirsts, come to the waters; and you that have no money, come, buy and eat! Come, buy wine and milk without money and without price ... Listen carefully to me, and eat what is good, and delight yourselves in rich food" (Isaiah 55:1–2).

- There is an invitation to *seeking, repentance,* and *forgiveness.* "Seek the LORD while he may be found, call upon him while he is near; let the wicked forsake their way, and the unrighteous their thoughts; let them return to the LORD, that he may have mercy on them, and to our God, for he will abundantly pardon" (Isaiah 55:6–7).

- There is an invitation to *mystery.* "For my thoughts are not your thoughts, nor are your ways my ways, says the LORD. For as the heavens are higher than the earth, so are my ways higher than your ways and my thoughts than your thoughts" (Isaiah 55:8–9).

- The invitations continue, but the root seems to be an invitation to a *life-giving covenant* with God. "Incline your ear, and come to me; listen, so that you may live. I will make with you an everlasting covenant " (Isaiah 55:3).

Jesus, who gave us a new covenant in his own blood (1 Corinthians 11:25), had a ministry that radiated invitations. In the gospel of John chapter 1, John the Baptizer tells his followers they should switch from Team John to Team Jesus. But when John's old crew approaches their new rabbi and start asking him questions, Jesus doesn't give them answers. He just extends an invitation: "Come and see" (John 1:39).

As the rumors about Jesus begin to spread, it's not long before someone doubts Jesus on the basis of his Podunk pedigree. When Philip tells Nathaniel about the Messiah from Nazareth, Nathaniel asks, "Can anything good come out of Nazareth?" (John 1:46). If Philip had been trained in modern thought, he might have tried to out-argue Nathaniel by vouching for either Jesus or his hometown ("Top Ten Reasons Why Nazareth is

Awesome"). But Phillip offered no answer and no argument, just an invitation: "Come and see" (John 1:46). Philip's response is beautifully unoriginal. By making an invitation, he immediately followed Jesus in the plainest possible terms.

In Matthew 11:28, Jesus invites others to rest in himself, saying, "Come to me, all you that are weary and are carrying heavy burdens, and I will give you rest." But does an invitational theology selectively ignore the difficult, confrontational teachings? Are we soft-selling the like-it-or-not commands of Jesus and watering down biblical commands into squishy suggestions? Not when kindness is the command and invitation is the example. Further, Matthew 22:1–14 contains a parable of party (another party!) and invitation, but it's also a parable of judgment. In Matthew 16:24, Jesus invites his followers into the deeper waters of discipleship, where "If any want to become my followers, let them deny themselves and take up their cross and follow me." Revelation 22, the last chapter of the Bible, contains these ethereal words: "The Spirit and the bride say, 'Come.' And let everyone who hears say, 'Come.' And let everyone who is thirsty come. Let anyone who wishes take the water of life as a gift" (v. 17). Another party. Another offer for the thirsty. In the end, another invitation.

As we begin to read the Bible as a book of inspired invitations, we can also begin to recognize that our lives and interactions with others have a similarly dynamic, Spirit-led quality. It's not just that inviting someone to a wedding is a teachable metaphor or that throwing a party is *like* the kingdom of God. It's that giving or receiving an actual invitation can be a way to build the *actual* kingdom.

At the very moment I (Jeremy) am typing these words, my toddler son has appeared at my feet. He's holding his new truck. He speaks no words, but he knows what he's doing. He is looking at me. He wants to play, and his very presence is an invitation.

I'll be right back.

Invitation Fail

Consider the worst invitations you've ever received. The misfire was probably not due to bad data: the incorrect day, time, or place. It was probably botched in the delivery and had more to do with the wrong attitude: obligatory, guilt-laden, chiding, desperate, needy, or commanding.

I (Jeremy) once got a gift I didn't want from a relative I didn't know. The relative stranger handed me a box and eyed me hungrily. No sooner had I torn the paper before they pounced, saying, "Now I'll be expecting a thank-you note for this." I never forgot that exchange, perhaps because there was a sense in which that gift never really left his hands. Some of us use wrapped packages as a mechanism for debt, a means of control disguised as a gift.

Generous invitation-making is not for control freaks because it guarantees very little to the inviter. Our invitations do not ensure a positive response any more than our giving a gift guarantees a grateful reception. We give, and the gift is out of our hands. In this way, the spiritual discipline of invitation is one way of crucifying our control issues. Of course, the phrase *control issues* occurs nowhere in the Bible. But the Bible does talk about self-control.

Self-control is an underrated, misunderstood, and interpersonally essential fruit of the Holy Spirit. When the Bible talks about self-control, it doesn't mean we should be stuffy or unemotional. At a minimum, self-control is control of *self.* So abandon those uptight stereotypes, and consider what self-control is *not.* It is not me controlling others. It is not others controlling me. And once we realize the degree to which we want to control others, or the degree to which we want others to control us, this one small word of truth single-handedly wipes out dozens of sinful, dysfunctional, relationship-wrecking behaviors.

So what does all this have to do with invitation? The spiritual discipline of invitation cultivates the spiritual fruit of self-control.

In making an invitation, we acknowledge that we cannot control others. We respect their free will because God respects their free will (and ours). We respect their power and right to choose just like God respects their power and right to choose. The human side of salvation hinges on our ability, willingness, and grace to receive a gift. We are not cajoled into resentful cooperation. We are invited to follow Jesus and live a resurrection life.

Both of us come from a Christian denomination that is historically opposed to violence on principle. It's not that we're unwilling to die; we're just unwilling to kill. And we didn't come to that position overnight. But there is a short distance between conviction and self-righteousness, and we are often tempted to fast-forward someone else's spiritual pilgrimage. We have a friend who says, "No one is chided into Christian pacifism." We'll go a step further and say that no one is chided into any aspect of Christian discipleship. Will others drag their feet when they should be walking the walk? Of course. We've done the same. But our impatience and heavy-handedness toward others is not only unnecessary, it also exposes our disbelief in grace. It isn't that severity is inappropriate. It's just often misplaced. Rather than twisting the arms of others, we should be driving the nails more deeply into the palms of our own control issues.

Inviting: Ten Non-Commandments

Invitation can take many forms, so here are ten practical tips on extending invitations in Jesus' name.

1. *Make It Golden*

Unsurprisingly, the Golden Rule works wonders. How would you want to be invited? Consider the best invitations you've ever received. Of course, they were accurate, but logistical accuracy ought to be the minimum standard. Were they well-timed? Considerate? Heartfelt? Did they have your best interest in mind? Go and do likewise.

2. *Ask and Give Space*

Don't say no for someone. "Oh, I can't ask them. They'd never agree to do that." Don't say yes for someone. "I just volunteered you to help with ..." Ask. Let them speak for themselves. And allow space for their acceptance or rejection.

3. *Make It Personal*

We are living in a world that is saturated with advertising and mass communication. The implications are tremendous, but the one thing we'll point out is that *proliferation* brings *desensitization*. The more splashy commercials, blinking pop-ups, and cartoonish junk mail we encounter, the more impervious we become to large-scale invitations in general. Not only that, if our churches attempt to use mass communication, we will find ourselves competing with the relentless noise machines of popular culture. To clarify: Use all the means you can to get the word out. Use attractive mailings, use social media, use TV commercials, use signs and banners and streaming video. Heck, use carrier pigeons! Just know that none of them will have the impact of an invested, personal, life-on-life invitation.

Although they look official, we question the effectiveness of invitational form letters sent from a church office. Instead, ask a friend to church and invite them to lunch afterward. If your church feeds the homeless and you have a friend who likes to cook food or grow veggies, ask him or her to pitch in. Of course, anyone we invite to anything has the right to ask, "Why are you inviting *me*?" And we'd better have an answer. But make it personal. We recently heard a college pastor tell his coed congregation, "You will probably have to invite people to *you* before you invite them to *church*."

4. Be Resilient

If you are a person who RSVPs quickly and attends faithfully every time your presence is requested, we have some bad news: you are not a normal person. I'm sorry you have to hear this from us. You are a stranger in a strange land. If you start making invitations, you'll quickly find this out.

Inviters have to be tough. We have to endure no-shows, last-minute cancellations, and flaky behavior that borders on rudeness. Our guests will agree to show up and then skip town if something better comes along. Some people are so phobic about commitment they won't even commit to coming to a party. Others are too disorganized, too distracted, or too complicated. Experience has taught us that some people are avoidant because they are hiding sin or shame. Many will offer no explanation. Rejection can be emotionally expensive, and inviters had better be prepared to pay the price.

If you are inviting someone to a task or project where that person's presence is absolutely mission-critical, he or she ought to know that up front. And if they stand you up or blow you off, you need to think twice before calling on them again. Of course, if your bestie bails out on you at the last minute, you have every right to ask them what happened—another advantage of a relationship. Otherwise, relax, carry on, and keep sowing the seeds. Strengthen your resolve, but don't harden your heart.

5. Volume Counts

If you want ten people to come to your event, you may have to invite one hundred. Personally. This is especially true if your congregation is a church plant, a new mission start, or a declining church that wants to turn around. It's probably true if you're launching a new program or ministry. Our friends who believe that "small is beautiful" find this tough to swallow, but it's true. In the remarkable book *What Every Pastor Should Know: 101 Indispensable Rules of Thumb for Leading Your Church*, Gary McIntosh and Charles Arn cite research suggesting that only one out of every ten persons invited to church actually shows up.

We wish there was a way to make this convenient, but there isn't. There are times when I (Jeremy) have sent thirty handwritten invitations to a Sunday school class I was teaching. We know one church that looks back longingly on the days when they had three hundred people in worship. What they forget is that their pastor at the time was officiating fifty weddings a year and personally reaching out to every single couple and family who tied the knot. We know too many churches who put forth a halfhearted invitational effort, and when only two or three people show up, they piously invoke Matthew 18:20, "For where two or three are gathered in my name, I am there among them." Obviously, we should make the best of any response, large or small. But please do not use Scripture as a poor excuse for a poor turnout. And if you want a big crowd, make an outrageously broad personal invitation.

6. *Master the Art of the Non-anxious Invitation*

Those who recruit volunteers (what one church calls "unpaid servants") in our congregations have a hard job. This is especially true if attendance slips and the talent pool shrinks or if your church has a governing structure from twenty years ago (when the church was twice its size) that is not proportional to current needs. More than a few committee meetings are spent trying to figure out how to "fill the slots" on the committee. Fatigued recruiters can easily slip into arm-twisting and guilt-tripping in order to get the job done. We recently heard some Christian teenagers refer to this as "volun-told," a strange mix of politeness and coercion.

Are you a concerned recruiter? Good for you. You're concerned because you care. Share your care, but contain your worry. Take it from us. If you don't, you'll only sound desperate and weird. And if your worry has grown into frustration and bitterness, please don't take that out on the church that loves you or the folks you are witnessing to. If you mix a gallon of ice cream with a gallon of manure, you'll end up with two gallons of manure. The same thing happens when we mix invitation and venting. It stinketh.

Our invitations wield spiritual power, so please be a good steward of that. In some churches, we've heard people say, "I knew I was 'in' when they asked me to serve in the kitchen." One person who was recently asked to count the offerings responded by saying, "Thanks for noticing I am trustworthy." A new believer who was asked to serve communion was blown away. One wise sister taught us that we need to remember that we are inviting people to "the joy of service," and that little phrase has changed our perspective. We don't have to be hyped and hokey, just be short and sweet and (if possible) *spiritual*.

Of course, there are times when urgency is called for. But don't push the panic button unless it's truly necessary. Otherwise, your church's proclamation about Jesus Christ may not be as memorable as the desperate public guilt trip during the announcement time.

7. Invite to Serve, Not Just to be Served

I (Jeremy) used to think that if Christians simply served their neighbors that the silent witness of our service would be enough to change the hearts of those we served. After all, everyone loves to quote Saint Francis, saying, "Preach the gospel at all times, and if necessary, use words." As it turns out, neither is true.

Of course, it's true that our words should match our actions and that Christian service is nonnegotiable. But our service by itself is not always convincing. Nor is it always helpful.

Sometimes we meet a real need, and sometimes we unwittingly enable those we serve. Some are satisfied with an imbalanced relationship and are quite happy to get free stuff forever. (Remember John 6:26?)

Ironically, there are times when unchurched and/or unbelieving people actually want to serve *with* us, not be served *by* us. Not everyone, of course, but there are those whose hearts are moved when they see Christians engaged in compelling mission. I (Jeremy) was once involved in a fantastic after-school ministry. Despite our efforts, those we served on Wednesday nights rarely connected with our worshipping community on Sunday mornings. But our church did grow with people who were looking for a meaningful place to get their hands dirty. We rarely turned "getters" into "givers." More often, it was our *giving* that attracted *more givers.* In another context, a local dentist approached me who it made clear that he was not a Christian. But as soon as he learned I was a pastor, he asked with excitement if we have any overseas mission trips planned for the near future. Why? "Because I love going with churches overseas and offering free dental work to those they are serving." Now that's an invitation!

If your church is doing service projects, and if you are not inviting your unbelieving and/or unchurched neighbors to pitch in, you're missing out. (And although we love that quote, Saint Francis never really said it.)

8. *Respect the Stakes*

There are work environments, family relationships, cultural sensibilities, interpersonal politics, private addictions, invisible allegiances, and individual histories that have the potential to raise the stakes of any invitation. We aren't suggesting for a second that you bow to every social pressure, but be wise and innocent (Matthew 10:16) and aware of them.

9. *Beware of Amenities*

This might sound strange, but stay with us. Plenty of Christians invite others to their church on the basis of their church's amenities. "We have great music, great preaching, and a great children's playground." Obviously, these are not bad things; we work hard to provide them. But if we invite others only on the basis of amenities, we are setting ourselves up to fail, and here's why. Once someone else comes along with better music, better preaching, and a better children's playground, we're in big trouble. We suspect this is why so many people bounce from church to church. They are making their membership, attendance, and participation decisions on the basis of superior amenities. Why shouldn't they? That's how they were invited!

Once this dynamic sets in, everybody loses and weirdness ensues. The underdog churches get tempted to overstate the value of the amenities they do offer. The conversation goes like this:

Someone says, "Church X down the street has such a great facility!"

We respond, with mild defensiveness, "Well, we have a great facility too!"

This comparison mind-set can create a kind of cold war within the kingdom, but what should we expect when we stop talking about God and start talking about stuff? By contrast, the top-dog churches can get trapped in an unsustainable quest for bigger and better. In our experience, at least some leaders are aware that their institutional supremacy is tenuous and temporary.

We hope your church has a great facility, but keep in mind that you also have a great God. (And please don't use that phrase, "we have a great God," as an excuse to not pull the weeds from your parking lot or as a reason to not refurbish a derelict nursery.) Consider making an invitation on the basis of "fit," something we'll talk about more in Chapter 7, "Finding Words."

10. Remember an Invitation Cannot Say It All

We've heard several wise people make a bracingly honest statement about human relationships. "If I would have known what I was in for, I never would have done it." This isn't a case of their having been deceived. It's also not a case of regretting disastrously poor choices. It's the reality that even the most beautiful endeavors can be fraught with more difficulty than we can possibly know at the start of the journey. And although we're glad we've done it, had we known with certainty all that the journey had in store, we'd probably not have taken the first step.

Should we count the cost? Weigh decisions carefully? Be informed and inform others? Absolutely. But there comes a point when we must jump. In our so-called Information Age, we do not suffer for lack of data. We suffer for lack of relationships. And if we are not courageous, we will die as lonely people, buried in content. Can an invitation tell us everything? No. But it gets us started. Invitation is a positive temptation, an incitement to jump. You don't have to say it all or know it all. You probably can't anyway. Just invite.

As I (Jeremy) write this chapter, a U-Haul truck has appeared just a few doors down from our home. I've been looking out my window, watching the family. I've not been asked to help, but how would they know to ask me? It's late. And it's hot outside. But the family looks a bit understaffed at the moment, and after all, I am writing a book on loving your neighbor. I'm going to go out on a limb (in faith?) and interpret the U-Haul as a cosmic invitation.

Hold on. I'll be right back.

Cardboard Cards and Greasy Spoons

Here are two true invitation stories.

Months after I (Jeremy) met Tos and Ken, I was called to serve an intriguing but struggling little church outside Seattle.

This congregation had begun decades earlier as a Bible study in a coalmine break room. Digging into the Word, they outgrew the break room and had to meet in a chicken coop. Growing further, they finally came together to build a meetinghouse from local lumber and stone. They filmed part of this church-raising and have real sepia-toned footage of guys with no shirts chopping down trees and lifting beams for the small chapel. Aside from modest ranchettes, the church was the only building in the area. But by the time I arrived, this forested backwater had transformed into a booming Seattle suburb. And during the same period, when the newly incorporated suburb experienced a 24 percent growth rate, the church property had grown derelict and worship attendance dwindled to almost nothing. Overtures were being made to sell the property. But, of course, if one was going to plant a church, this would be a superb location. The potential was thrilling, but the obstacles were daunting.

We needed to find a way to get the word out and invite others but had no idea how. We had zero dollars for a direct-mail campaign. I'd had some experience designing creative brochures when I pastored in Indiana, but Seattle (even the suburbs) was different. Anytime I tried to give someone a brochure about my little church, they recoiled as if I were trying to poison them. I also had a background in neighborhood ministries, but doors were slammed in my face.

I felt stuck ... until inspiration struck.

Seattle speaks green. The region is beyond environmentally friendly; all the cool kids compost. And what you know can be less important than who you know. Networking is a way of life, and I've almost never seen anybody refuse a business card or an invitation to coffee. One day when my wife and I were at one of Seattle's raucous, creative street fairs, I saw a small vendor who used handmade business cards made from corrugated cardboard. Cut with a razor and stamped on both sides, it was an outrageously low-budget and green-friendly way to go. I knew we had to give it a try. (If some of you are groaning at the tree-huggers, all I can say is you're not an uptight Seattleite.)

I started devising ways to swindle old women in the church into wielding Exacto knives and slashing up cardboard, but a better door opened. A wonderful new family had started attending the church. They were eager to help and owned a small paper-cutting business. In mere minutes, they produced stacks and stacks of little cardboard cards, all from cardboard headed for the dumpster. Little icons of redemption.

But what could we say on the cards? Something theological? Something proud and historic? Something peppy and upbeat and inspirational? It all felt phony and pretentious because we weren't a normal church. The people in the newly budding congregation certainly wanted to grow closer to the Lord and reach out to its community, but it was looking to me for direction. The building itself was certainly distinct, a quaint patch of sacred space surrounded by towering Douglas fir trees. But the whole scenario was also absurd in more ways than one. We had no means to impress anybody, and we were across the street from McDonald's and Hot Yoga. I believed in the power of the gospel but couldn't take our situation seriously enough to make a convincing sales pitch.

We settled for the basics. On the card, we stamped the church name, address, phone number, website (we finally got a good one), and worship times. And on the bottom, we stamped these two lines:

Between McDonald's and Hot Yoga
(We think it's funny too)

We didn't need a sales pitch. All we needed was an invitation.

This was no tract. We weren't laying out the metaphysics of atonement, parsing Greek verbs, or curating a doctrinal statement. It also wasn't pretty. We didn't use stock photos of happy white people on the beach holding their arms up toward the sunset. We were extending an invitation and doing it in a way that was genuine to who we really were. We gave them away by the hundreds. Honestly, we were surprised at the reception. One person examined them closely and said, "Hmm ... this is so off-kilter. Homemade, funny, unpretentious, and earnest. It tells me everything I need to know about your church."

We're not telling you to go forth and make cardboard cards. We're telling you to make invitations in the native language of the people you're called to reach and teach and in whatever way is genuine to how God is making your community of faith.

The second true story, which takes place far way from Seattle, involves a guy named Clem. He was a truck owner and operator whose fleet of dump trucks hauled gravel and asphalt. He lived by himself in the country, was known for being playfully cantankerous, and began most days at the local diner in town. Another guy named Jake frequented the same greasy spoon. Jake was a salt-of-the earth family man who worked for a construction company. After two years, Clem and Jake became friends and enjoyed exchanging barbs with each other in a spirit of good-natured, macho harassment.

One day, in slightly more serious conversation, Clem told Jake that he had not attended a church since his preteen years. He emphatically proclaimed the church as a rigid, uncaring club that existed only for Goody Two-shoes. More quietly, he let slip that someone in his old youth group many years ago had hurt his feelings. Jake listened before responding gently but plainly, "My church isn't like that. We have people from all walks of life, the good, the bad and the ugly." Sensing an open door, he said, "Clem, why don't you give it a try?"

Clem said sheepishly, "If I'd show up, the roof'd cave in!" Both men laughed, but the invitation immediately weighed on Clem. For several silent minutes, the truck driver seemed to take a strong interest in cleaning his fingernails. He finally took a sip of coffee and said, "Jake, I'll make you a deal. If you show up at Hooters on Thursday night around nine o'clock and have a drink with me, I'll consider your invitation." They left the table as friends but with an agreement that made both men squirm.

Jake kept the date and met Clem at the bar. Clem was stunned and didn't try to hide it. For his part, Jake was white as a sheet and couldn't hide it if he wanted to, having grown up in a home so dry his parents refused to patronize grocery stores that sold alcohol. As Jake sat on the barstool beside Clem, the two friends fell back into their groove of exchanging playful barbs. Jake drank Pepsi, and his nervousness slowly dissipated. He felt he had done right by holding up his end of the bargain.

Clem, on the other hand, dragged his feet for weeks. He probably never would have come to church with Jake had not Jake offered to pick him up and go for breakfast together. Jake also had to assure Clem several times that casual dress was okay. When the Sunday morning formally arrived, Clem greeted Jake with the words, "Okay, let's get this over with." He wasn't joking.

When they arrived at the church, a few other regulars were getting out of their cars and noticed Jake was bringing Clem to church. As they walked to the front door of the church together, one of the men said, "Watch who you keep company with, Clem!" He pointed to Jake. "He'll lead you astray!" Clem smiled nervously and said, "He already has."

Clem didn't consciously hear much of the sermon because he was too preoccupied watching other people and making sure he didn't make a fool of himself. His experience of the church's hospitality was almost unnerving, as the genuine smiles and kindness directed at him made his defenses feel unnecessary. He didn't want to enjoy the experience, but despite himself, he did. A follow-up invitation from Jake established the new ritual for Clem.

Whether Clem gained a newfound faith in Christ or whether he picked up where he left off years ago is hard to tell. But Clem unloaded some old hurts, changed some old habits, and was baptized in the church he thought he'd never enter. And today, Clem would say that Jesus is his Lord because Jake is his friend.

Chapter 7
FINDING WORDS

Emergency Call

Maria was told, "In case of emergency, call Tim." And now she was calling.

Between Maria's broken English and Tim's poor hearing, it was difficult for Tim to understand exactly what was wrong. She didn't seem panicked, but it was clear the matter was urgent, so Tim scrambled his team and bolted for Maria's home, thinking, *This can't be good news.*

Tim was a member of Cedar Hills Church. A year earlier, Cedar Hills decided to sponsor a refugee family from Latin America. Tim was newly retired and liked helping people, so he volunteered to head the committee that would provide for the family's needs. Maria was a single mom with two young children and had never been outside of Colombia. Their needs were considerable.

But both Tim and Cedar Hills excelled at every step. They found a modest but well-maintained house, arranged for English lessons, provided transportation, job training, and even some meals. Cedar Hills was a conscientious congregation that didn't want its kindness to come with strings attached, so the congregants decided at the outset to downplay their religious affiliation. Besides, evangelism was something of a sore spot for their congregation. More than a few of their members had joined

Cedar Hills after leaving other churches they felt were too pushy, and many people prided themselves on being "not like that." Service was their sweet spot.

Not only had Maria never attended worship at Cedar Hills, she had also never called Tim's cell phone. Until now. As he drove a little too fast, Tim ran through a mental checklist. "Was it the water heater? Something with Maria's family back home? Or, God forbid, the kids?"

When Tim pulled into Maria's driveway, he was relieved to find no police cars or fire trucks. When he knocked on the door, it was silently opened by several of his fellow committee members who had arrived before he did. Assuming they had already received the bad news, Tim tried to gauge the severity of the situation by reading their somber faces. There was some combination of frustration and awkwardness as they gathered in the kitchen, but he sensed no distress. Tim adjusted his hearing aid before asking, "Maria, are you okay? What's going on?"

She was standing. "I need to tell you something. It's about a man named Jesus. He is God's Son, and God sent him to Earth to save us and show us God's love." Tim noticed the tract Maria was holding. "Some people came to my house and told me about him. He died, but then he came back from the dead. For us!" Her face was radiant. "Now I have decided to follow Jesus. I asked him to forgive me. You have done so much for my family, I wanted to tell you about Jesus so you can follow him."

Tim flushed. He didn't want to be offended, but he was. And when he spoke, there was more of an edge to his voice than he intended. "Maria, we're already Christians! We're a church group. Why do you think we are doing all of this?"

All eyes were on Maria. Her radiance quickly faded, and her brow furrowed in confusion. Now it was her turn to feel hurt. She set the tract down on the table, looked at the group of servants gathered in her kitchen, and asked, "Then why didn't you tell me?"

Although we've changed the names, the story of Tim and Maria is true. Cedar Hills was and is a gracious, generous, service-oriented congregation. No one could describe them as judgmental. And in their push to not be pushy, they were solving what was, for them, an irrelevant problem.

We recently heard one pastor say, "I agree that we should collect our bottles and cans and cardboard as part of our discipleship and part of our stewardship of God's earth. But it's not enough for us to just recycle and then expect our neighbors to come up to us and ask, 'Why are you recycling?' This is especially true when our acts of charity don't look all that different from any other service group. *Demonstration* is vital, but at some point, we have to get around to *proclamation*."

Richard's Words

It seemed like Richard was always on the church property. He drove a beat-up truck, had a tireless work ethic, and could fix anything. A contractor by trade, he loved working with the building and grounds committee, often humming hymns as he worked. He also had a background in teaching and had a knack for mentoring both adults and children.

In contrast, Joel had never been to church in his life except for weddings and funerals. But his DUI conviction meant that he had to do forty hours of community service, and Joel had heard that churches could provide easy work. Joel called twelve different phone numbers before he found a congregation that would agree to work with him. When Richard explained to Joel, "As long as you show up on time and don't mind getting your hands dirty, we can start tomorrow."

In less than seven days, Joel had logged thirty hours of community service at the church, most of it side by side with Richard. As they began their second week of work together, Joel's curiosity got the best of him. He leaned on his shovel and asked, "Rich, why are you doing this?"

"Doing what, Joel?" Richard asked, still shoveling.

"Working here with me," Joel replied.

This was not Richard's first rodeo. Unbeknownst to Joel, Richard was also a recovering alcoholic. He could sense where the conversation was headed, so he patiently went along with it. "Uh, don't you need community service hours?"

Joel stepped away from his shovel. "No, I mean, you don't know me. You don't know what I've done."

Richard kept digging as he talked. "Joel, I don't have to know. It's none of my business. Lord knows we've all done things we shouldn't have."

Joel forgot his shovel altogether, increasingly perturbed and fascinated by what looked like the foolish charity of an old man. "But you don't know what kind of person I am. I could be a really bad guy, and you've just wasted all this time helping me out. You don't even know my last name." Joel was smiling, but he was serious. By now, so was Richard.

The contractor finally put down his shovel before saying, "Joel, our church wants to help. And we're willing to help people before we know them, and whether they deserve it or not. That's what God does. I'm giving you this help and showing you this hospitality because I believe God is love."

In Place of Formulas

Maybe you've noticed that there is a lot of prepackaged evangelism paraphernalia on the market. We're not talking about testimonies or teachings. What we mean are formulas, scripts, procedures, techniques, methodologies, and manuals that tell you to "say it just like this."

Many Christian leaders tell us that such a formulaic approach does not make for good evangelism. We are told that faith-sharing scripts are oversimplified, dumbed-down, clichéd, and ineffective. Not only do they lack theological integrity (because they are reductionist or trite), they just don't work. But if this is true, why do they abound?

It's tempting for us non-formula users to bypass this question entirely and consider ourselves spiritually superior for not using them. But mindlessly rejecting formulas may be as dangerous as mindlessly embracing them. Perhaps we should ask, What itch do these formulas scratch? When we (Fred and Jeremy) followed this question, we were surprised where it led us.

Most of us know people whose *confidence* exceeds their *competence*. This pertains to all areas of life, including evangelism. Sometimes the most willing are the least able. Many of us have encountered recklessly self-assured sisters and brothers who would do well to temper their witness with the Hippocratic oath, "First, do not harm."

But increasingly we find brothers and sisters whose *competence* exceeds their *confidence*. They do not stumble in walking the walk, but they fumble in talking the talk. We have a friend who has a beautiful story of genuine life transformation in Christ, but he's terrified of telling it. He told us bluntly, "I'd rather give a lot of money to my church than talk about my conversion." And he does.

The more folks like this we encountered, the more we began to wish that somebody somewhere would come up with something to help. Can't we invent a pill or an energy drink that would give people a surge in evangelistic confidence? Something that would boost their morale and banish the Jesus jitters?

That's when we realized that one such tool has already been invented: formulas.

Who doesn't want to know exactly what to say to the seeker, skeptic, or prodigal? We certainly do. What principled Christian doesn't want to be assured that the answers they give are absolutely faithful to Scripture? We want that too. And if an evangelistic product, script, or formula can assuage my fears and put certainty within my reach, we're certainly in the market for it. Formulas scratch the itch of our own self-doubt. But in the process, something vital is lost.

A religious script works wonders for my confidence; it gives me a persona of strength and something to rely on. But that confidence is misplaced. We are asking people to place their trust in Jesus while in the same breath we are placing our trust in formulas, scripts, procedures, and manuals. We recently heard a friend say sardonically, "Love is too scary. Perfect *formulas* cast out fear."

We (Fred and Jeremy) have friends doing amazing ministry in Haiti, a country where voodoo has a tenacious hold on the lives of the people. The belief in voodoo is so embedded in the Haitian psyche that when Haitian pastors encounter problems in their ministry, they often turn to voodoo for the solution. We're told that some Haitian pastors will pay a voodoo priest to cast a spell that will make the church grow! This appalled us, until we saw the log in our own eye. For too many of us, techniques and methods serve as a kind of voodoo. We believe in them. We know they work (or think they do). And relying on them is what bolsters our confidence. Formula worship is a subtle and seductive idolatry.

But what are we supposed to do with our self-doubt? With our uncertain words? Are we to expose our plain, non-formulaic willingness to believe with all our heart in an unprovable gospel?

Catherine's Words

Catherine has known the Lord since childhood. From her earliest years, she has no conscious memory of unbelief. But she clearly recalls a conscious choice during her first year in college.

At the university, she met a fellow student who challenged her faith. He liked to argue and believed atheism was the most scientifically feasible perspective. Catherine had no problem reconciling both faith and science in her heart and mind, but her fellow student rejected her reasoning. When Catherine quoted Bible verses, he was unmoved. When Catherine asserted her personal sense of God's presence, he brushed it off as a psychological miscue.

Later, when alone, she said to herself, "Okay, Cath, this is the time to really decide for yourself. You're away from home now, and it's up to you to think this through."

Although she never left campus, the next few days were a pilgrimage. One of the primary questions she wrestled with was "Can I prove this?" When she finally reached the crossroads, she felt there was no way for her to prove God's existence or nonexistence in the absolute sense. She came to realize that her atheistic challenger also had a kind of faith. While he was not religious per se, he had a great deal of confidence in unprovable assertions. She finally settled on the defining statement, "Choose, and think about where that leads you."

Catherine never convinced her classmate, but the challenging exchanges forced a remarkable growth within her. Like roots plunging into the soil, her faith grew deeper in ways that no one could fully see. It was one of many experiences that gave her a hard-won steadiness. But like a canopy of branches, her vocabulary of faith extended with grace and breadth. She was justifiably more confident in her expressions, engaging but not defensive, centered and substantive.

By the end of the semester, she knew she had crossed some kind of invisible spiritual threshold, an experience she could only describe as "some kind of divine hug." And although she continued to grow in Christ throughout her life, this crucible informed her faith, her words, and her perspective for the next five decades.

She also went on to marry a science teacher.

Necessary, Not Ultimate

In a completely unscientific survey, I (Jeremy) recently asked dozens of my believing friends about how they verbally expressed their faith to people who disagreed with them. I posed this question to young'uns and oldies, red-state Christians and blue-state Christians, all people I respect, all brothers and sisters whose example in Christ I want to emulate in some way. I had hoped to come away with a handful of helpful expressions or a poignant turn of phrase. Instead, I was blown away by three common responses.

First, almost every single person said he or she found it difficult to articulate his or her faith with those who believed differently. Remarkably, those who *did* come from strongly evangelistic backgrounds expressed about the same reticence as those who *did not* come from strongly evangelistic backgrounds. One person who privately confessed a twenty-yearlong distaste for evangelism had, in the same period of time, served as a missionary overseas.

Second, most people told me stories of how they shared the gospel with others or how others shared the gospel with them. In every instance, faith sharing involved loads of listening, long relationships, multiple conversations, genuine caring, and as one person said, "Time, time, and more time."

But the third common response was the most surprising. When it came to their faith sharing stories, *no one could remember the exact words that were used.* When they shared the faith with others, or when others shared the faith with them, my friends could easily recall the relationships that were built, the resistance that was felt (from within or without), the time that was spent, the books that were read, the churches that were involved, and the acts of service that were done. And while in every single instance faith sharing involved words, there was no identifiable phrase, line, pitch, or conversation that drew them or anyone else to Christ. At least not that they could remember.

All this led me to ask, What if all our words are *necessary* but not *ultimate*?

We know this is a potentially dangerous question. And we're not telling you to wing it. What we say matters, so choose wisely. [3] "The word of the Lord endures forever" (1 Peter 1:25), so ground your words in Scripture, in the Spirit of Christ, and in the truth of Christ. But consider that your witness may not rise or fall on the strength of your syntax. What if finding the words to use was not as important as simply finding the courage to speak? Before we agonize over our exact expressions, it's worth remembering that our words might not be remembered.

But if our words may be forgotten, why say anything at all?

On April 21, 2013, a young woman named Justine was shot to death by her boyfriend in her apartment. She was twenty-four years old. Justine's killer then went on a shooting spree in the apartment complex, gunning down three other people before he was killed by police. This story made national news.

Seemingly out of nowhere, I (Jeremy) was asked to lead Justine's memorial service. I had only met her once, in passing, without any conversation. The multiple murders were so surreal, evil, and unimaginably cruel that everything about them was hard to convey. I have rarely felt the failure of language so severely.

Preparing for Justine's funeral was no small task. But when I learned that her father was also going to speak at the service, I knew that my role paled in comparison.

On the day of the funeral, when her father took to the podium, he seemed to be shaking. He began by saying, "Words are not enough. But sometimes words are all we have."

---

[3] Note: While no one could remember the exact words that were used when it came to *positive* evangelism experiences, it was quite the opposite in the case of *negative* evangelism experiences. My friends could remember with striking and uncomfortable clarity the insensitive responses and bad theology that others had inflicted upon them.

Officiating Justine's service was a severe honor, and it shaped me in several ways. But it was her father's words that became my synopsis for any Christian testimony. It is as true of tragedy as it is of glory: Words are not enough. But sometimes words are all we have.

A Word about Words

I hate not knowing what to say. Proverbs 25:11 says, "A word fitly spoken is like apples of gold in a setting of silver." But scarcely is the fruit of my mouth so shining, polished, and well-placed. More often, my words feel inadequate, squishy, ill-fitting, and stupid. The loathing of my own speechlessness goes far beyond eulogies for murder victims. I hate not knowing what to say at birthday parties. I hate not knowing what to say at mechanic shops and sports bars. The common denominator, for me at least, is that words are so *personal*. So when my words fail, *I* fail. When my words are inadequate, *I* am inadequate. And when I stumble in the attempt to express my most deeply held values, I feel like I have failed the very cause I most believe in. Silence seems safer.

Sometimes silence *is* better. There are times when talking spoils everything. When I asked one excitable, extroverted friend how he shares his faith with others, he told me, "First, I shut up." There are all kinds of situations in which words are unnecessary. Sometimes the best response is no response. Both depravity and beauty can take us beyond the edge of our expressive powers, and this is as it should be. But silence also makes us squirm. We fill uncomfortable voids with unnecessary verbiage. I am guilty of smothering mystery with my own anxious sermonizing. But I am learning, slowly, through failure and through Scripture, to be still. When I am able to do that, I am amazed at how God's inscrutability speaks for itself in wordless reverberation.

But in both silence and in speech, I have also come to this troubling realization: When I avoid talking about my faith, it is usually not because I am honoring a holy moment. When I evade proclamation, it is usually not because I am being a good steward of stillness. More often, I am trying to protect my fragile ego and prevent myself from looking foolish. What if I am rejected? What if I am misunderstood? I silence my testimony, witness, and story not because it is better but because it is safer.

Chongan's Words

Chongan is a writer, and his wife is a painter. They live in Blissville, a funky neighborhood known for its artsy boutiques and bohemian vibe. Chongan is also a leader in his local congregation, a new, small, experimental church with great music. Surveys show that Blissville has the lowest rates of church attendance of almost any neighborhood in the United States, and studies have been done about the local population's seemingly allergic reaction to organized religion. But because Chongan knows Bilssville firsthand, he sees what the statisticians don't: the unofficial religion of his neighborhood is a mix of skepticism and cynicism. And as Chongan's pastor likes to say, "Cynicism is a wound disguised as wisdom." In his neighborhood, Chongan knows he has about three seconds to make some kind of faith-friendly statement before he is completely dismissed. So when the topic of faith comes up, he often begins with gentle confidence. "I'd rather be a believer than a skeptic."

Befriending Speechlessness

Words fail. Even in the attempt to share the gospel, our language will fall short. But maybe we should treat this like a good thing.

Perhaps we should befriend our own speechlessness. It can bring us to the end of ourselves. It may even be a sign that we are on holy ground. Here's how:

1. *Speechlessness can clarify the object of our faith.*

As a friend recently reminded me, "Faith has an object." And while I will always do everything I can to express my faith in a way that is understandable to the hearer, *I do not have faith in my own words.* I do not have faith in my powers of expression. My vocabulary is not the object of my faith. My faith is in the loving, resurrecting power of Jesus Christ, in who he is and what he does.

Not knowing what to say can make us feel inadequate. But what if this inadequacy, while bad for our ego, is good for our soul? My words are not doing the work because they were never intended to. Jesus has done the work. The Holy Spirit is doing the work. I am not called to be an orator; I am called to be a disciple. So I lend my voice, even though I have no real confidence in it. My words about Jesus are an insufficient offering, a crude finger pointing to a beautiful moon.

2. *The failure of our language highlights our need for the church.*

We can't say this enough: following Jesus is a team sport. And because you are probably not the star player, passing the ball is not the same thing as passing the buck. Is your testimony stale or stuck? Ask an articulate, considerate friend at church how they talk about Jesus (this becomes an exercise of fellowship and discipleship, by the way). Invite a seeking person to have coffee with your articulate, considerate friend from church (this becomes a way to build their relational connection and belonging to the body of Christ). Our words may not be as important as our network.

3. Not knowing what to say can open our hearts anew to the Word of God.

The next time you feel speechless, read these words from the apostle Paul:

> When I came to you, brothers and sisters, I did not come proclaiming the mystery of God to you in lofty words or wisdom. For I decided to know nothing among you except Jesus Christ, and him crucified. And I came to you in weakness and in fear and in much trembling. My speech and my proclamation were not with plausible words of wisdom, but with a demonstration of the Spirit and of power, so that your faith might rest not on human wisdom but on the power of God. (1 Corinthians 2:1–5)

The person who has an answer for everything and is constantly protected by ironclad confidence simply cannot identify with what Paul is talking about. An honest understanding of our own verbal shortcomings does not disqualify us from being a spokesperson for the truth. In fact, the Bible is filled with people who tell God they cannot tell people about God. Consider:

Moses: In Exodus 3 and 4, God calls Moses to be the point man to bring God's people out of Egypt. Despite a concert of miracles, Moses is so convinced of his own inadequacy that he finally says, "O my LORD, I have never been eloquent, neither in the past nor even now that you have spoken to your servant; but I am slow of speech and slow of tongue" (Exodus 4:10). The Lord's response? In short, the Lord didn't let Moses escape with an excuse.

Isaiah: In a dreamlike, bizarre, inexpressible vision, Isaiah saw the Lord. And what was Isaiah's first response? His tainted life and lips. "Woe is me! I am lost, for I am a man of unclean lips, and I live among a people of unclean lips" (Isaiah 6:5). The Lord's response? To forgive Isaiah and then to call him as a prophet.

Jeremiah: When God called Jeremiah to be a prophet, Jeremiah's first words were about the insufficiency of his words. "Ah, Lord GOD! Truly I do not know how to speak, for I am only a boy." The Lord's response? A command (to speak), a calling (to go), a promise (of presence), and a placement (of divine words in a human mouth) (Jeremiah 1:6–9).

None of these guys were speech majors. None were self-assured. All were called in spite of their (dis)qualifications. It's almost as if they were called to serve in the very area of their weakness.

4. *The failure of language can demonstrate the power of weakness.*

What if accepting Christ included accepting our weaknesses? Yes, I am inadequate. Yes, I fail. With humility and trembling, I am going to open my unqualified mouth for the sake of my inexpressible God, and I am probably going to get it all wrong. But when I embrace my weakness rather than attempt to cover it or compensate for it, I may find weakness itself is not a problem. It may even be the beginning of the solution. In Christ, our weakness can be a witness.

Ben's Words

Ben is a cabinetmaker by trade, an introvert by nature, and a Christian by choice. He, his wife, and his teenage children are regulars at their Baptist church in rural Oregon. He hates being the center of attention, but because of his deep love for Christ, Ben recently started pushing himself to share his faith with others. In the process, he rediscovered the obvious: he is good with wood but not with words.

When it became clear to Ben and his wife that their preteen daughter was anorexic, they were devastated. Their little girl was slowly killing herself. And Ben felt like he was dying with her.

Ben's friends and coworkers knew something was wrong. Ben refused to pretend everything was fine, but he knew it was inappropriate to share the depths of his anguish with most people. He also wanted to maintain some semblance of privacy for the sake of his daughter's recovery. His friends at church were his lifeline. And there were times when both he and his wife knew the only thing keeping them sane was their nightly prayers together as a couple, even though it was usually a tearful mess of total desperation.

Although his relationship with God was now more important than ever, Ben also had fewer words than ever to express it. Witnessing in any form seemed absurd. So when people asked, "How are you doing, Ben?" the only honest thing he could do was to swallow hard and say, "We pray a lot."

For those who knew Ben, those four words were more powerful than a dissertation.

Nine Tips on Talking

If you're a seminary professor, an experienced Sunday school teacher, or a believer with the gift of gab, you may not need this section. But for the rest of us, here are nine practical suggestions for finding words to share your faith.

1. Find openings, demonstrate openness

This goes hand in hand with finding words. Christians often dismiss small talk, but when we do, we can miss some of the easiest ways to probe a person's heart and mind. Movies, music, television, viral videos, politics, and any number of other topics can be natural connecting points when it comes to faith. Move beyond the question of entertainment value (was it funny or not, etc.) into engaging the content, the spirit, or the questions they raise.

We have one friend whose approach to faith sharing has undergone a radical transformation. She shared that she no longer thought about evangelism as funneling someone toward a specific outcome on a specific timeline. These days, she says, her conversations are "far more my asking others what they believe rather than my offering what I believe." This interested inquiry creates a give-and-take openness and a respect that keeps all parties from being guarded or defensive.

2. Engage the "operational theology"

This is a pretty sophisticated idea, and it doesn't originate with us. But we think it's important enough to try to understand.

Everybody has a theology. We used to think Christians had theology and non-Christians didn't. Now we believe everybody is living some kind of theology whether they realize it or not. Even if a person has never read a theology book in his or her life, knows nothing about Christian doctrine, or is not fully aware of it, he or she still has a spiritual framework he or she believes in enough to act upon. This isn't what we say we believe; this is the theology implicit in our living. For lack of a better term, we'll call this "operational theology."

Take my friend Gerard (not his real name). Gerard works hard. Long days, long nights, Gerard takes care of business. From the outside, all we can see are his actions. But whether he realizes it or not, Gerard is actually driven by the idea, "If I work hard, everything will be okay." To say that he is a zealous worker is a literal statement. Work is his creed, his faith, his theology. He could self-identify as a Christian or say he's a Zoroastrian; it doesn't matter. His operational theology is defined by his own personal effort.

Take another example from the world of romance movies. The formula is familiar. Boy meets girl, stuff happens, but eventually boy and girl fall in love. Their world is complete, they will be together forever, and they ride off into the sunset. (There's usually a sex scene somewhere in the mix too.) Often, the message beneath the plot is that romantic love equals redemption. Nobody comes out and says this, but their actions show what they really believe. To be alone is hell. Heaven is where boy and girl are "together forever." The film may never mention God, but that storyline contains the operational theology "eros saves."

This is a big idea to cram into a short space, but we wanted to introduce it. We also wanted to offer some questions that might help us engage the operational theology in the lives of those around us:

- *Who, or what, saves?* For some, it is their personal initiative. For others, it is a boyfriend or girlfriend. Political candidates are often elevated to the level of saviors, or we may have our own Messiah complex and want to somehow deliver others. It can be more education, a better economy, a workout program, or a gun. We've heard "product evangelists" describe manufactured goods in a way that is positively rapturous. What is the person or the thing that rescues us from the ills of ourselves or of the world?

- *What are we serving?* Is it our ambition? Our own creature comforts? A cause that we have elevated to an ultimate status?

- *What causes the sin and brokenness in the world?* Often this question is answered in a wistful statement that begins with "If we could just ..." For example, "If we could just come to a better understanding of science, all this would go away." Or, "If we could just get this political party out of office ..." Or, "If we could just get my ex-husband out of the picture ..." The forces we blame are often what we have come to understand as the root of all evil.

117

Perhaps this sounds abstract. But pay attention, ask questions, and listen for when people you care about express an implicit religious framework. Look for times when a friend's operational theology collides with their experience of the world, like when Gerard the workaholic has an accident and can't work anymore ("How will I be okay if I can't go to work?"). And when the time is right, engage someone's operational theology with a better, more biblical, more gospel-centered theology.

3. Ask about family

Long ago, Fred gave Jeremy this advice: If you want to know about someone's spiritual life, ask about his or her family. Our families shape much of our foundational identity and often provide the source of our greatest hopes and deepest pain. It is no mistake that the Bible expresses our relationship to God in familial terms.

We have one colleague who counseled and befriended a man for over a year. While the man did not appear to have any major problems in life, he was consistently evasive on the topic of his father. Eventually, it became known that the avoidance was born from agony. The shattered father-son relationship was excruciating, defining the identity of the grown son. When our colleague gently probed, "What do you think God wants for your family?" and provided some answers of his own, that became the catalyst for healing, transformation, and Christian discipleship.

To inquire about one's family often reveals a great deal about one's operational theology. We know people who have demonized their family, and we know people who worship at the altar of their family. While living in the American West, I (Jeremy) have met too many people who simply abandoned all their relatives back east and moved as far west as they could. They felt their family was the root of all evil, that their freedom required an exodus, and any address west of the Mississippi was the Promised Land. There is an unmistakable theology to this kind of behavior.

We're not saying this is easy territory, but if you have enough relational credibility to talk with someone about it, the impact can be deep and lasting. There might be a reason for the familial language of the Bible: the Savior of the world, God's Son, our brother, brings many children to glory (Hebrews 2:10–13).

4. Move from big ideas to specific definitions

We have a friend with the spiritual gift of evangelism. Her advice? Talk about love. The reason? Everybody thinks they know what love is, and everyone experiences the failure of human love in some form. Further, the Bible talks explicitly about God's love in Jesus Christ so there is plenty of material to share. Substantive conversation about the big idea (love) can naturally lead to sharing about how Christians understand God's love in Jesus.

This applies to other big ideas as well. Who doesn't care about life? About trust? About hope? About freedom? Listen for the big ideas that others care about, and talk about them. But don't stop with affirming abstract nouns. Let meaningful conversation about these heart-touching themes move from the general to the biblically specific.

5. Ask (and answer!), "What does that lead to?"

We know several people who use this question to profoundly beautiful effect. As they hear others share about their hopes, dreams, plans, and hurts, they often ask, "What does that lead to?" One woman we know asks, "Does it lead to wholeness?" which, of course, includes a spiritual dimension. To simply ask this question is wise. But if our conversation partner then asks us the same question, we are often presented with an opportunity to share our perspective, a pertinent Scripture, or the hope that is within us. At best, it can be an invitation to a turnaround, the beginnings of a call to repentance.

6. For church, focus on "fit" (not amenities)

In Chapter 6, we gave the advice "Beware of Amenities." By this we mean that Christians should be wary of making invitations to church based solely on attraction-based bells and whistles, such as "We have a great children's play area" or "We have a killer band!" This amenities-driven invitation is especially out of place if you're in the middle of a deeper discussion. You don't want to be in a conversation about the pain and suffering of the world and suddenly say, "And come to our church. We have three food courts!"

Sure, invitations to church could start with amenities if need be, but we hope you don't stop there. If possible, try to reframe the invitation in terms of "fit." By "fit" we mean a kind of spiritual chemistry, a discerned compatibility, the discovery of a spiritual match between community and participant. Obviously, this depends a great deal on your context, but it can be a beautiful and powerful thing. Following are two examples:

First, we have a friend who adopted two incredible children from Ethiopia. When she moved her family from one coast to the other, she needed to find a new church home. She visited one congregation, seemingly at random. She was surprised when she discovered that this medium-sized church had families that included over a dozen children adopted from Ethiopia! She told us, "I could find a church with a bigger nursery or a slicker children's program, but why? This is where we fit."

Second, we know one church with a high rate of chemically addicted people. On any given Sunday, at least 60 percent of those present have been touched by alcohol or drug addiction. This was not the result of intentional outreach to the recovery community. It simply happened. The pastor of this congregation had a warm, relatable style and regularly followed up with first-time guests in worship. Newcomers would regularly confide in him about their own addictions or the addictions of family members. This provided the opportunity for the pastor to say, "I'm not at liberty to say exactly who is struggling with what, but if you make our church your home, I can promise that you won't be alone in your struggles. And I can promise you'll be welcome."

You'll probably never see Ethiopian orphans or drug addicts used as selling points on a church brochure or website. But these are the tangible and intangible characteristics of a faith community that can make for a fit. Of course, a genuine spiritual chemistry between member and body should go beyond demographic similarity ("Come to our church. We have all white people!"). It may even go beyond like-mindedness ("Come to our church. All of us vote the same way!"). It should be based on the healthy, mutual, divine give-and-take in the body of Christ.

If you're looking for a church home, ask yourself: Is this a church that needs my service? Is this a group of people who can help me grow closer to the image of Christ? If you're talking with someone who is looking for a church home, rather than saying, "Come to our church. We have great (fill in the blank)," what would happen if you said, "I am at this church because God wants me to belong here. What kind of church do you think God wants you to belong to?"

7. The four "Whys?"

Give this little drill a try. Answer the following four questions, using only one sentence per question. And imagine that you are answering these questions for a person who is not a Christian and does not have a church home, so use terms that religious rookies would understand.

1. Why Jesus?
2. Why my congregation?
3. Why my denomination? (If you don't have a denomination as such, answer the same question of your network, affiliation, or nondenominational association.)

4. Why you? (The unchurched, non-Christian person you're talking to)

Pastors, what if you gave this little assignment to your congregation on Sunday? What would it reveal? Could the responses be used on your church's website? As a future teaching series? And would it help your church be able to share their faith better?

8. Time, Heart, Word

One friend recently shared with us that many short, personal stories of faith often contain three ingredients: time, heart, and Word. In this case, "time" refers to a chronology, a point or series of points in history. "Heart" equals vulnerability, a need, a hurt, or a problem. And "Word" means the Bible, the Word of the Lord. Consider the presence of time, heart, and Word in the following two true testimonies.

- "I had been sick in the hospital for weeks. There was one woman I knew who would come and visit with me. She was full of life and love for the Lord. She would read me short Bible verses to lift my spirits. I hated it. And I hated her, even though she was kind and generous toward me. But when I got home from the hospital, and she kept bringing food to my home, I finally broke down. I saw a light in her that I lacked, and I started to follow Jesus."
- "I grew up with a vague idea of Christianity, but I was definitely not a believer. Then I went through a time of severe depression. I went to bed one night, having made up my mind to kill myself in the morning. I even had the pills to do it. I don't share this with many people, but I had a dream that night. In my dream—I hope you don't think I'm crazy—Jesus appeared to me. I saw him push back some kind of evil force. I don't even know how

to describe it. He told me he loved me, and that I was his child. I woke up knowing that I had been changed somehow, and I flushed my pills. I started looking for a church home. I hear a lot of people talk about how they got 'saved,' and I know the Bible talks about that too. But when I say I was 'saved,' I mean that literally."

Time, heart, and Word. While there is nothing magical about this, it can be helpful to remember if we're pushing ourselves to find words for our faith.

9. Jesus saves

At some point in our conversation with others, we need to talk about Jesus. That conversation can take many forms, and it can be years in coming, but it needs to come. This should be obvious, but sadly, it's not, so we (Fred and Jeremy) are going to risk offending people we care about and take no prisoners on this one.

Talking about your fantastic congregation isn't enough.

Talking about your cool pastor isn't enough.

Talking about your earth-shattering, this-changes-everything ministry philosophy isn't enough.

Promoting your awesome denomination isn't enough.

And nondenominational folks, you aren't off the hook either. Promoting your awesome nondenominational network or awesome independent status isn't enough.

Passionately advocating for your faith-based cause or charity isn't enough.

It's not enough because it's not Jesus.

We belong to a particular denominational family. We are advocates of the local congregation. Our networks, frameworks, movements, and affiliations can be an excellent way to serve Christ. But if Jesus is truly Lord, Jesus must come before everything, even the things that are meant to serve him.

It doesn't matter if our church is in a cycle of boom or a cycle of bust; it doesn't matter if our pastor is a keeper or a loser. Our church is not God, our pastor is not God, our denomination or nondenominational movement is not God, our doctrinal statement is not God, our ministry philosophy is not God, I am not God, you are not God.

Too many of us think we are witnessing for Christ when all we're really doing is giving a commercial for our tradition. We think we are sharing the good news when all we are doing is sharing the mixed bag of organized religion generally. Being an ambassador for Christ must not stop with making a case for our institution, however good that institution may be. Church-worship does not save. Church-bashing does not save. By God's grace through faith, we find salvation in Christ alone.

Perhaps we should audit our endorsements. It could be the case that our evangelism exposes our true gods. That is, we may find that the things we are *actually* promoting are the things we *actually* believe in.

You may well find yourself in a situation where a seeking person asks you to explain the reasoning behind your church membership or wants to hear more about the discernment that went into your choice of a denominational family. That's great. But the bigger question, and the one we'd better be prepared to answer, is, What is it about Jesus Christ that the world cannot live without?[4]

Words fail. But sometimes, so does silence.

---

[4]   We owe this question to Tom Bandy and Bill Easum.

Chapter 8
EMBRACING RISK

Holy Terror

I (Jeremy) grew up washing feet. My parents were and are faithful believers and solid leaders in their small, rural Brethren congregation. Our tribe regularly gathered in the church's concrete basement to reenact the Last Supper by singing hymns, hearing sermons, sharing a plain meal, taking communion, and washing feet. After all, Jesus said, "If I, your Lord and Teacher, have washed your feet, you also ought to wash one another's feet" (John 13:14). I have held the basin and towel for my elders, and I have seen those same elders unhesitatingly bow, stoop, and assume the posture of a servant at my feet. Those memories are powerful, positive, and electric.

Several years ago, my wife and I visited a friend who was serving a large Christian church in Bangkok, Thailand. Far from the Midwestern American cornfields of my upbringing, Thai culture has a distinct view of the human head and feet. As I understand, Thais see the human head as a sacred thing. It is taboo to so much as touch someone else's head. Barbers apologize to their clients before they begin cutting hair. On the other end of the spectrum, Thais perceive the human foot as something almost profane. Pointing with the foot or toes is beyond rude, and it would be wildly disrespectful to touch anyone—or any important object—with your feet. Even to step on discarded newspaper could be considered insulting, especially if that portion of newspaper included someone's photograph. It's just like stomping on their head. With Thailand's tropical climate, regular foot washing is a necessity, especially considering many people wear little more than thin, plastic flip-flops as they make their way through dirty city streets, dusty hill-country roads, and sandy beachside trails.

One day, while relaxing barefoot in my friend's Bangkok apartment, I asked if his congregation would ever wash feet as part of a worship service. It was hard for him to even consider it. "Never. It would be too uncomfortable, too countercultural, too insulting, too much for people to bear. It's just too risky."

His response was disappointing but understandable. After all, I have a long history with ritual foot washing. Now every new experience of foot washing makes a deposit into an already full bank of worshipful memory. But there is a downside. For me, the power of this act is not necessarily in its audacity, but in its nostalgia. I am not shocked, threatened, or uncomfortable at the prospect of giving or receiving a foot washing. I break no social taboos, I feel little vulnerability, and I unhesitatingly bow and stoop, in part because I know I have little to lose. I am warm to the idea because I am numb to the shock.

In this regard, I am different from others in my own culture, most of whom consider foot washing to be awkward, odd, or threatening. Some are uncomfortable with the touch, the intimacy, or the exposure. Some are simply unfamiliar with the experience. Jesus wasn't Thai, but he wasn't American either. And the first-century Mediterranean cultures had a view of feet—and foot washing—that is far more Thai than American. For many Americans, foot-washing reticence is about the mundane indignity of sock fuzz and toe jam. For many Thais, foot washing represents the descent into the profane. They cannot wash feet without losing face. The whole business is inherently risky.[5]

Not long ago, a woman named Kelly started attending our church. Kelly researched our congregation for three full months before she walked in the door for the first time. She read online announcements, listened to my sermons on the Internet, and did some digging on our denomination. When she told me this, I tried not to be nervous ("I wonder what she read …?").

But before she began googling churches, Kelly came to Christ in a remarkable way. She did so alone, on her knees in her living room, overwhelmed by the weight of her life. She reached out to Christ for redemption, and then she reached out to us for community. Music to my soul.

It wasn't long before Kelly told me, "I want to get baptized. I'm ready to commit. What do I do?" I explained, in simple terms, that there were two aspects to baptism at our church. "First, there is the spiritual aspect. Baptism is a public confession of faith, representing a death to self and sin while also rising to new life in the name of the Father, the Son, and the Holy Spirit. Second, there is the logistical aspect. We're going to dunk you in a tank of water. And because our hot water heater is broken, it's not exactly going to be a baptism by fire."

"I'm going to go through with this," Kelly replied, "but I'm terrified." I expected as much. I've done enough adult baptisms to know it evokes not only the fear of the Lord but also the fear of accidental drowning. In church. At the hands of one's pastor. But I still asked, "What part are you terrified about? The spiritual part or the logistical part?"

"Both, but especially the spiritual part. I'm going on record. I used to tell myself, 'I don't need a church in order to be a Christian.' But now I know that was all justification, self-protection, and an

---

[5] You've probably noticed the foot-washing scene on the cover of this book. For the whole story, go to e3ministrygroup.com

excuse. Before when I screwed up in my Christian life, there was no one to see me. Now people will see me, and everyone will know what I'm supposed to represent."

I have come to see that all of those Bible words, all of those Jesus words, are *all* risky. Faith? Hope? Love? Don't kid yourself, they are dangerous, every one. Overfamiliarity is a vocational hazard for churchy types like me; we can easily become sedated by tenure. But those on the outside looking in, people who are afraid of commitment, freaked out by trust, and skeptical of relationships, they know better. Kelly is not oversensitive or skittish. She is more mature than she realizes. I know this because she is acutely aware of the inherent riskiness of following Jesus.

We need to resensitize ourselves to the inherent risk of following Jesus.

Where Did All the Miracles Go?

We are blessed to have friends and family from a variety of Christian traditions. These sisters and brothers often save us from our own blind spots and limited vision. They see things we don't. For example, take my Pentecostal and Charismatic buddies. They are quick to point out that when it comes to miracles, the Bible and the church often don't look alike. Listen to Scripture, and the Bible booms with signs and wonders. Listen to sanctuaries, and crickets chirp. I used to think of my Spirit-filled siblings as effusive, enthusiastic, well-meaning believers who were also selective literalists. (Don't tell them I said that.) But over time, their plain reading of both text and church really got me thinking. Where did all the miracles go?

I am beginning to believe that the glaring absence of the miraculous is linked to the conspicuous absence of risk.

Try this: Find a miracle in the Bible, and see if you can also identify a corresponding risk or threat that necessitated the miracle.

Miracle: The parting of the Red Sea
Risk or Threat: The Egyptian army coming in for the kill

Miracle: Manna from heaven
Risk or Threat: Starvation in the desert

Miracle: Jonah in—and out—of the whale's belly
Risk or Threat: Nineveh's destruction

Miracle: Jesus healing the sick
Risk or Threat: The illness itself, and the drain
on life and livelihood that the illness caused

Miracle: Lazarus raised from the dead
Risk or Threat: Unbelief

Miracle: Jesus' resurrection
Risk or Threat: Death

We're not saying that every biblical wonder absolutely required a risk, but there does seem to be a connection between the miraculous and the perilous. What's the point of parting the Red Sea if there is no Egyptian army?

And what does all this have to do with your church?

Some of my Pentecostal and Charismatic sisters and brothers freely confess that their tradition, at its worst, has made an idol of miracles. Fair enough. But I suspect that many more of my brothers and sisters, across Christian traditions, have made an idol of safety.

A Strategic Choice

Here are two true stories. On the surface they have nothing in common. But they share a subterranean similarity: they are strategically self-protective.

First story: When I was a teenager, friends of my parents invited me to a special evening worship service at a neighboring church. The invitation came because a Christian college choir was going to be performing (and recruiting) at this service, and our friends knew better than me about the power of Christian higher education. But choir music? University brochures? I thought the whole thing sounded painfully boring in a good-for-you kind of way until I realized what was really at stake: college girls. On a normal day in our slow, small town, such prospects were nonexistent. When I saw this for the opportunity it was, I jumped at the invitation and dressed to impress. My short haircut, buzzed almost to the skull, required minimal primping. I was ready in a flash, and all parties nodded approvingly at my veneer of virtue.

When we walked into the sanctuary, my immediate realization was twofold. First, no college girls. Second, darkness. While not mood lighting per se, the space was uncomfortably dim, which created heavy, grave atmosphere.

Before my eyes had adjusted, a strapping, warty, beast of a man swiftly approached me. Although he was serving as a greeter, he had the look and disposition of a person who could successfully be cast in role of an orc in a *Lord of the Rings* film. Although we were complete strangers, he grabbed my head with his meaty paws and bellowed, "Boy, I like your haircut!" I was terrified. He released my head only to take hold of my earlobe with his thumb and forefinger, rumbling, "So long as you ain't got no earring." Somehow he managed this violation of personal space without ever making eye contact.

Second story: A married couple, let's call them Bill and Gina, are successful, young, attractive professionals in the Baltimore area.

130

Both are committed believers, faithful servants, and genuinely hospitable. They drive immaculate cars and dress impeccably. A few years ago, their church was in decline.

Bill and Gina's church got a new pastor, a woman we'll call Sally. When Sally began to address the church's troubles and talk more about the necessity of outreach and faith sharing, Gina and Bill seemed to take the lead. Not only did they encourage fellow members to leave their comfort zones for the sake of the kingdom, Gina and Bill also immediately began inviting others to church.

As a direct result of Bill and Gina's efforts, their church saw a steady stream of money-poor, burned-out, down-on-their-luck, drug-addled people. So Gina and Bill practiced what they preached. Sort of.

Pastor Sally was grateful for this power couple, but she privately wondered, "How are Bill and Gina so adept at making interpersonal connections with people so unlike them? Why are they so successful at reaching 'unsuccessful' people and so unsuccessful at reaching 'successful' people?" It was a sad, obvious reality that many of Bill and Gina's invitees never stayed connected with the church for long. While the church was kind to them (an accomplishment in and of itself), their lives were too chaotic to maintain any meaningful long-term relationship. But Sally kept this concern to herself and wondered if she was overthinking things.

Until one day there was a confession. Sort of.

It came when Sally and Gina were working together, assembling a servant evangelism project for their church.[6] Alone in the church basement, they spoke in the unguarded, comfortable way that people do when their hands are busy. After some time, Gina said, "I'm so glad we're doing this. Bill could never talk about God at work." This caught Sally's attention, and she asked, without much thought, "Really? You and Bill both seem capable talking about anything with anybody."

---

[6]   More on servant evangelism in Chapter 9.

Gina continued, hands still moving, "Oh well, it's not about capability. It's just, you know, the economy."

Sally sensed alarm bells going off but kept her composure and probed quietly, "The economy?"

Gina, still in motion, said, "You know how it is. People at work, at the country club. You spend your whole life working hard." An uncomfortable picture was emerging, and Sally felt anxiety rising within her. Gina concluded, "I feel so much better helping poor people. And you can talk to them about Jesus without any risk to your career."

Gina and the creepy greeter are two very real, very different people. On the surface, they have nothing in common. But they actually share one important characteristic: risk management.

Gina and Bill are the sort of members many churches say they want. They are resourced, enthusiastic, dedicated, and genuinely kind people who give words to their faith without being overbearing. In terms of the rich reaching out to the poor, they seem to set a sparkling example. But the deeper reality was that they would not put themselves in a position to lose one ounce of face or iota of upward mobility. Privately, they had assessed the risks and capitalized on the power differential between themselves and those they reached out to. Their selective hospitality was a strategic choice.

As for the scary greeter who manhandled my teenage cranium? Think about him for a moment. This guy was possessed of sufficient confidence, extroversion, and bad boundaries as to seem fearless (including fearlessness about being sued, but that's another story.) His willingness to invade my personal space in the near-darkness was profoundly intimidating to me. But he was intimidat*ing* because he was intimidat*ed*. As tempting as it is to dismiss this incident as an innocent social gaff, no one else that night was the target of his bombast. As much as I would have disbelieved it at the time, I am now convinced that *he* was afraid of *me* … or he was afraid of who he thought I was, or who I might be, or what I unwittingly represented to him. He was less like a greeter and more like a gatekeeper. And his choice to express hostility disguised as hospitality was a strategic choice as well.

They understood the risks. They counted the cost. They just weren't willing to pay the price.

Necessary Foolishness

Perhaps we are not as courageous as we'd like to believe. A friend once told me, "I like our pastor because he's not afraid to offend people in his preaching." But the people this pastor stridently, fearlessly affronts also happen to be people who are his and his church's ideological enemies. They are a target of convenience. I have colleagues who agitate for agape, saying, "Jesus said we should love our enemies!" But in many cases, my colleagues are preaching to the choir. They are not talking about loving *their* enemies; they are telling their enemies to love *their* enemies. Again, zero risk involved. Perhaps the truth is that all Christians are selective literalists. We select the truths that are safest for us.

We are not advocating reckless impulse or poor planning. We are not saying that offending people or not offending people is always an accurate spiritual barometer. What we are advocating is mission over preservation. We are advocating principled, intentional, cost-counted risk for the sake of God's kingdom. In a word, this is faith. And if we will embrace this kind of peril, even in small doses, God may just come through with the miraculous.

John caught my eye the first time he walked in the door of the church. He was intent, guarded, handsome, and had a big Bible in tow. He entered and exited, quickly and quietly. When I asked him to coffee, he replied, "Later. I'll let you know when it's time." The suspense was killing me, but I waited. Six months later, he said, "It's time."

It turns out John was a long-time Christian, an unemployed computer programmer, a former leader in his former church, and a recent divorcé. He poured out his story to me over breakfast in a crowded local restaurant. "I was one of those guys who insisted I'd never get a divorce. Never. Then I got a divorce." It was wrenching to see such a cautious man come to tears in public. "I can't go back to my home church. I know what they do to divorced people. I've seen them publically rebuke divorcees. And I've been a part of it myself." As he outlined what this poor treatment involved, I was stunned. Then his voice quivered. "My heart has been shredded. But your church seems like a safe place." I assured him it was, no longer trying to fight back tears of my own.

He continued in a very different direction. "Since I'm trying to put my faith and my life back together, I did something foolish, something I never would have done before."

Here goes, I thought.

"About eight months ago, I was driving by a homeless guy on the street, and on a whim, I stopped and talked to him. I gave him a few dollars, prayed with him, and offered to meet with him again. I know this sort of thing never works, and I had no hope for making any real change in his life, but my life was in shambles so I made the offer anyway."

Deep breath.

"Well, it worked. We've been meeting about once a week to talk and pray. I bought him a cell phone so we could stay in touch. I helped him get a job, even though I am unemployed. I also paid the first month's rent on his apartment. His life isn't perfect, but he's off the street." Then John said, "I feel really fortunate."

I'm glad John didn't ask my advice before doing something so "foolish" because I know what my advice would have been. "Your direct efforts won't accomplish much. Leave this to the professionals. Give some money to a homeless shelter, go home, and take care of yourself." But it turns out John's foolishness was—and is—more necessary than I imagined.

A friend of mine in Virginia, let's call him Todd, pastors a big suburban church. Todd recently learned that the director of a

well-known, urban, homeless rescue mission started attending his
congregation. So Pastor Todd arranged a meeting with the director
and asked the obvious. "What can our church do to support your
rescue mission? A fund-raiser? A coat drive? Recruit volunteers for
the soup kitchen?" The director replied, "Well, Todd, between the
two of us, our mission has plenty of supplies, plenty of volunteers,
and plenty of money. I don't share that widely because we don't
want our donors to dry up, but it's the truth. What we really need
are people who are willing to form meaningful relationships with
the homeless. Just be a friend. But nobody wants to do that."

Well, John did. And against all odds, it worked. Almost like
a miracle.

Stories of Audacity

We have one friend who, under the right circumstances, tells his
testimony in terms of the multiple miscarriages he and his wife
have endured. He lays out the bad advice and terrible theological
counsel they received and the words that only multiplied their
suffering. It is no small feat that his heart, soul, mind, and strength
have survived. While not exactly unscathed, he shows passion
without bitterness. Following this series of valleys, shadows, and
death, he is unwilling to stand on top of the pain of others
and make grand pronouncements. There is no oversimplified
sensationalism, no saccharine-sweet answers, no bullheaded
bluster. And he wins a hearing from people who disagree with
him because they recognize and respect his unmasked pain.

We have friends in three radical congregations whose mission
is to live alongside the poor. This is no feel-good addendum to a
conventional lifestyle. It is who they have chosen to be. In each case,
the congregation itself is closely connected to or overwhelmingly
made up of people who are homeless, prostitutes, drug-addicted,
mentally and physically handicapped, or just struggling to meet

basic needs. Body odor and awkwardness abound. But in each case, these churches are thriving, in part, we think, because of their unapologetic audacity. While attending a worship service with them, we noticed several middle-class families in attendance (they were impossible to miss). We spoke with one particularly square-looking dad who told us, "I am here to teach my kids. I tell my children that we go to this church because our discipleship is not about us. God's grace is enough, so church should not be about what we get. Church should be about what we give." In the other two congregations, the metric of success is not how many people attend their worship services but about how many people choose to move into the poverty-stricken, drug-addled neighborhoods in which the parish is located. If this sounds like a lot to ask, that's because it is. And it is their sustained, unhidden nerve that is more convicting and convincing than the best sales pitch.

Let's be clear. Not everyone is called to be a chaplain for Hell's Angels. There will always be a place for vital ministries in seemingly mundane contexts. It's obvious that popular culture worships at the altar of sensationalism, and it's true that Christian faithfulness includes plain ol', boring ol' reliability. Just showing up and staying true is an accomplishment.

But no one is called to gutless neutrality. No one is called to self-preservation by practicing the lowest common denominator of vaguely Christian niceness. Jesus said, "For those who want to save their life will lose it, and those who lose their life for my sake will find it" (Matthew 16:25). We would do well to ask ourselves two questions: How am I trying to save my own life? How am I losing my life for Jesus' sake? These are radical questions, and they apply to all of us. Radical discipleship is, by God's grace, within our grasp and within our sphere of influence right now. We have a good friend who says, "Study the Bible in small groups. Then go out and do the most radically Christian thing you can imagine." Your grandma can do this.

Make friends, love people, share Jesus.

An Invitation to Foolishness

This is a book about relational evangelism. And if it's not been made clear yet, we'll say it here just in case: There is no way to make any relationship 100 percent safe. There is no way to make evangelism 100 percent safe. Add them together, and you've got a double-whammy of potential risk.

It's risky. Got it?

And now our unambiguous advice is this: take the risk.

We have a mentor who says we have basically two choices in life: to be a coward or to be a fool. The coward is willing to count the cost but is not willing to pay it. The fool exposes him- or herself to ridicule by throwing him- or herself wholeheartedly and outrageously against the unlikelihood of making any difference at all.

You're a fool if you try, and you're a coward if you don't. Take your pick.

Sometimes being "fools for Christ's sake" (1 Corinthians 4:10) just feels like being a plain old fool. The Bible is bursting with "before and after" stories, tales of peril and faith that paid off. But much of our life is lived between the "before" and the "after." It is the "during" that requires enduring. And sometimes outrageous courage.

We are asking you to be fools. We are asking you to take the risk of building meaningful relationships with people who are not part of your faith community and to reach out with unscripted caring toward people who are noticeably unlike you. We are inviting you to risk disappointment, failure, and stress. We are inviting you to risk rejection. We are inviting you to leave your comfort zone and put words to a faith you will never be able to fully capture. We are inviting you to risk your time, money, and energy in an effort that may not have any measurable payoff. We know that also means we are inviting you to potential pain, and that is no small thing. Sometimes it will be easier than you expect. Sometimes it will be harder than you expect. Count the cost.

And then, after you've counted the cost, *pay* the price.

Bonus:

Chapter 9

SERVANT EVANGELISM

This chapter is not about relational evangelism. In fact, this chapter is pretty different than the rest of the book. But, hey, that's why it's a bonus!

This chapter is about what we call "servant evangelism."[7] In relational evangelism, the relationship is the context. In servant evangelism, *the service* is the context. Here's a true story of what it can look like in action:

> "I got very turned off toward God and the church by things that happened in my childhood. Sunday school seemed to me way too strict, and my father would punish me if I complained too much about having to go. In my mind, I formed this image of God as a very bad-tempered, demanding dictator. I wasn't sure if he was real or not, but if he was, I sure didn't want any part of him. After I got out of high school, I refused to go to church for anything except weddings and funerals.

---

[7] In our minds, the person most closely associated with this type of outreach is Steve Sjogren, and we acknowledge our debt to his pioneering ministry.

> "When I was in my late twenties, my wife and I moved into this community. Our second child was born that year. My wife wanted us to attend a church, but I wanted no part of it.
>
> "We started doing volunteer work in this church-based soup kitchen downtown. We volunteered on Mondays, the same day that three people from another smaller congregation were all helping. One of them was a man in his seventies, and he was very impressive because of the compassion he showed for the people we served and because of the interest he showed in each of us. Over a period of time, I found myself becoming open to Christ again because of his influence. While he stood out, the other two were also kind and obviously didn't believe that God was a heavenly tyrant. We didn't join the church those people were from, but they are the reason my faith was renewed and that we started attending a church as a family near our home."

Think about this. The guy who said he was unwilling to give God or church another try was more than willing to pitch in with a church-sponsored soup kitchen. Sounds crazy? It happens all the time. We need to stop thinking of evangelism and service as two separate things and start practicing them together.

If you're not sure how to get started, try this simple and potentially life-changing devotional exercise. Take a walk or drive through your neighborhood. Then read the following:

> What good is it, my brothers and sisters, if you say you have faith but do not have works? Can faith save you? If a brother or sister is naked and lacks daily food, and one of you says to them, "Go in peace; keep warm and eat your fill," and yet you do not supply their bodily

needs, what is the good of that? So faith by itself, if it has no works, is dead. But someone will say, "You have faith and I have works." Show me your faith apart from your works, and I by my works will show you my faith. (James 2:14–18)

Sit down at your local coffee shop or library, and take a look around you. Now read this:

For I was hungry and you gave me food, I was thirsty and you gave me something to drink, I was a stranger and you welcomed me, I was naked and you gave me clothing, I was sick and you took care of me, I was in prison and you visited me ... Truly I tell you, just as you did it to one of the least of these who are members of my family, you did it to me. (Matthew 25:35–36, 40b)

Go to a strip mall parking lot, to a high school baseball diamond, or to a local park. And then read these words:

But Jesus called them to him and said, "You know that the rulers of the Gentiles lord it over them, and their great ones are tyrants over them. It will not be so among you; but whoever wishes to be great among you must be your servant, and whoever wishes to be first among you must be your slave; just as the Son of Man came not to be served but to serve, and to give his life a ransom for many." (Matthew 20:25–28)

Do this by yourself. Do this with a group. But don't just do it in your head. Do it with your body physically located in a place where you can see and be with others.

Then get to work.

Seek and You Will Find: Needs, Hubs, and Partners

If you're starting a service evangelism project from scratch, one way to go about it is to do some homework on needs, hubs, and partners.

Look for the needs. Our neighbor's need may be our church's mission. What does your community's problems or brokenness look like? If we take a servant mind-set, another person's tribulation is our opportunity to see and serve Christ. Sometimes we don't have to go across the world; we just have to go across the street. Here are a few examples:

- We know one church whose neighborhood was designated by city planning offices as a "recreationally deficient zone." Upon learning this, the church launched a series of opportunities for free, safe play for neighborhood kids.

- Another pastor was called to an aging, historic church in a small midwestern city. He quickly connected with local officials and got his hands on demographic studies. He was surprised to learn that there were an unusually high number of incarcerated women whose children lived in the homes immediately surrounding the church's facilities. Thinking of Matthew 5:26 ("I was in prison and you visited me") he started calling other area pastors and working on a plan to reach out to these families.

- We know of one booming suburban community in the Southwest that appears to have it all together. Families are active in schools, landscaping is immaculate, and homelessness is invisible. But the problems are hidden beneath the surface. Teen drug use is high (the result of plenty of money, time, and little oversight), domestic violence among adults is also very high, and a large network of spouse-swapping swingers thrives in a neighborhood that is packed with churches.

Perhaps the needs are obvious. Perhaps they aren't. But take time to look, and don't look alone! The process of seeking the broken places in your community is best done with a group of people who watch and pray together through the process.

Look for the hubs. We think of a hub as any place where people come and go. What are the gathering spaces, the marketplaces, the social centers in your area? Is it the local greasy spoon, the hipster coffeehouse down the street, or the teen-friendly, open-all-night fast food restaurant? Are there retirement centers, low-income trailer courts, or apartment buildings? Is there a college nearby? Is there a small group of preteen boys who ride their bicycles to the local park? Are schools a vital part of life in your community? How about sporting events? Are you in a drive-through neighborhood, a commuter culture where people in vehicles race past your church's facilities? In this case, the highway is the hub. We know of several suburban housing developments that are loaded with teenagers, but if you took a walk down the street, you'd never know. They are all inside, plugged in to the Internet and video games. In this case, the hubs are still very real. They are just invisible, electronic, and virtual.

Know where people go, gather, and flow. Then park yourself in one of these hubs for a day (or longer). Talk to the regulars. Take officials out for lunch, pick their brain, and ask their opinion. Find out where the needs are and ways they might be met.

Can you pass out bagels or donuts to students on the college campus? Can you pass out drinks to the frustrated commuters at the stoplight along with a humorous note about road rage? (Obviously, road rage isn't funny, but humor can do a lot to chill us out.) The opportunities are endless and should be customized and relevant to the context. Whatever it is, pick a project and get moving.

Often churches want to create hubs. We want to offer events based at our facilities, such as a widow's support group or a fair-trade coffeehouse, and that's great! But don't neglect the power of joining an already existing hub. In so doing, you can follow one of the most-spoken, least-heard commands of Scripture: go.

Look for the partners. This is one of the most overlooked, undervalued, under-leveraged aspects of neighborhood ministry. Who are the people who are already seeking to address the needs in your area? And how can you know about, network with, and learn from them?

We find that many churches are oblivious to the good works happening right under their noses. Maybe it is the social service agency, food bank, or library just around the corner. We know neighborhoods that have Catholic convents and Protestant intentional communities, and sometimes they are looking for partners in mission. In some cases, your potential allies will not be organized groups but informal, caring individuals who are already busy making a difference. We know of one impoverished neighborhood that was anchored in part by a single generous (and similarly impoverished) retired widow. This homebound, elderly woman somehow found a way to help almost every person who came to her door. Her social networks and relational credibility were enormous. The kingdom of God was quietly at work on her front porch and in her living room. We know of several families who have "adopted" the children in their neighborhood. They invite kids over for snacks, games, and play time with adults who will look out for them. What if, rather than buying more toys for the kid's play area at our church (an idea we support, by the way), we helped equip families that were already doing ministries like this?

Work like this is probably already happening in your community. The Holy Spirit is like that, working miracles everywhere. How can your church partner with the kingdom work that the Spirit has already initiated?

Priming the Pump: Twenty-One Ideas and Fifty Feet

Below are twenty-one ideas for servant evangelism. Before we get to them, we'd like you to understand four things. First, there are situations that you will want to seek permission from appropriate officials, but don't let that slow you down. Get permission, and get moving! Second, this list barely scratches the surface of possibilities so don't stop here. Go online, read more books on the topic, find out what churches in your area have done. Third, this list represents a spectrum of risk, commitment, and time. You don't have to jump into the deep end of the pool, but jump in somewhere! And finally, we'll tell you now: they won't all work in your neighborhood. This statement isn't a disclaimer as much as it is a ministry philosophy and core conviction that one size fits none. Your church is unique, and it's supposed to be, so experiment your way forward, adapt, adjust, and find what fits.

With all that said, here we go!

1. *Provide free gift-wrapping* at a store or shopping mall.
2. Provide some *food or drink* at a place where people gather or pass by. Go to a school, ice rink, beach, intersection, shopping mall, or transit station. Offer hot cocoa or cold drinks, and don't charge. As much as we believe in home cookin', you may need to use prepackaged foods in some form.
3. Provide *teddy bears to kids* at hospitals.
4. Hold a *community egg hunt.* This can be as simple as a few dozen plastic eggs in the grass or as elaborate as dropping

thousands of Easter eggs from a helicopter. We've seen both used to great effect.

5. Celebrate *May Day by taking flowers* to people who are shut-in.

6. *Parties* can work wonders. Hold a barbecue, a car drive-in, block party, homemade ice cream event, or a mini water park. Go for a creative or unusual theme and advertise it well.

7. We've done *sidewalk chalk art contests*, where kids are given a parking space to decorate and every kid gets a prize. We know churches that have invited children to build huge *cardboard castles*, using duct tape and large boxes discarded by local businesses. You can build them in the church's front yard, a community courtyard, or other public gathering space.

8. We know some churches that host *farmer's markets* on their property. This is no small commitment, but it can also make a big impact.

9. Hosting *community gardens* has become a popular way for local congregations to reach out.

10. Start or join a soup kitchen, food pantry, or other *hunger-related ministry*.

11. *Open your facility* to the community. We know many churches that host Boy Scout, Girl Scout, or Cub Scout troops. We also know churches that host Alcoholics Anonymous or other recovery-community groups. Get creative, and keep an open mind. We know churches that host counseling offices, thriving arts centers, and medieval reenactment societies. But remember: we aren't called to be just landlords! Make friends with the people who use your space, and invite them to join in appropriate service projects.

12. Take a *missions trip or learning tour,* locally or internationally. And don't just invite people from your church! Invite your

whole network, such as Boy Scout troops or Alcoholics Anonymous groups that use your facility.

13. *Mentoring programs* for at-risk youth.

14. *Support groups* for new moms, recent divorcees, or grief groups for those who have lost a loved one.

15. *Athletics groups* can still be a relevant ministry of the church, especially if there are none in your area. One room, one block of time, and one person who is passionate about workout programs like yoga, Pilates, or P90X can be all you need. By all means, try conventional sports like basketball, but don't be afraid to do something usual. Try street hockey or fencing. We know one large church that has three different men's groups that go target shooting. We know of one small church that, with very little planning (but LOTS of communication and publicity), initiated a community-wide Frisbee golf club. They meet on Fridays at midnight and involve over one hundred young adults!

16. Work with Habitat for Humanity or another *housing-related ministry.*

17. *Alternative Christmas celebrations.* Offer nonviolent toys, partner with fair-trade groups (like Ten Thousand Villages) and alternative gift-giving charities (like Heifer International).

18. Make *sock balls for the homeless.* On a recent summer trip to Denver, we found several churches doing this. They would collect several cases of new white socks along with plenty of hotel or sample sizes of hygiene items (toothpaste, toothbrushes, shampoo, soap, lotion, etc.). Just roll a pair of socks together, and stuff them with the hygiene items. Driving through Denver, we encountered plenty of panhandlers at stop signs. We'd roll down the window and hand them a sock ball. We never had to go out of our way, and they looked

relieved every time. As with many projects like this, the genius is in its simplicity. Not only is it easy to assemble and distribute, collecting the items can be a way to partner with others. Is your church building located close to a dentist office that could donate a case of toothpaste samples? Ask. And remember, the point is not to "get the stuff" but to create a connection—even with the dentist!

19. We recently interviewed a minister who told us that his community was struggling with high rates of alcohol-related violence. The local authorities were desperate for a solution and had already built a relationship with the church's leadership, so they asked if the church would be willing to help. The church took on this task by sending people to be physically present in the entertainment districts at peak party hours (evenings and weekends). Their motto and mission was "Listen, Help, and Care." They carried bottles of water, looked out for seriously inebriated people, and called cabs. They never gave out tracts but were always ready to talk with someone about faith if it was brought it up. Obviously, this was an intense project. But every night they had the opportunity to share their faith, and their efforts made a statistically measurable impact, reducing the rates of alcohol-related violence by 15 percent.

20. If you're going to do a giveaway, don't hand out cheap junk. You'd be surprised how many churches do. Tacky is bad. So is ugly. And while it may be affordable, items made by people working in uncertain labor conditions in the developing world will send the wrong message. We are huge fans of the Cambodian bells offered through Church World Service. These extremely rustic, radically repurposed, handcrafted bells are fashioned from spent shell casings and other scraps

of war. Use them for Christmas events, for themes related to peace, recycling, or redemption. They tell a great story, make a great handout, and at thirty cents each they should keep your finance committee happy. Go to http://www.cwsglobal.org/ and do a search for "Cambodian bells."

21. *Give them your card.* There is nothing wrong with giving someone a small card that explains who you are and what you are doing. Our advice: Keep it short, sweet, and sharp. Include your church name, address, worship time, website, or other social media links. Make it pretty, witty, or wise. Don't use a forgettable, cookie-cutter template. Make it stand out. Use ink stamps on recycled cardboard, form unusual shapes (triangles? origami?), and go for something homemade and handmade wherever possible. Include a clever one-liner that's appropriate for your project or a thoughtful phrase that links your action to your faith, such as "This bottle of water is a gift of grace, just like God's love."

Ideas abound. So how will you know what ones are right for you? We think it comes down to context.

Joshua Longbrake writes, "You will most likely never hear about the people who are doing the most good in the world. They probably don't have a blog. They're not on Facebook or Twitter. They're not writing books. They don't care about marketing themselves, their organization, their church, or their company. They aren't looking to box up their system in order for others to do the same things they're doing. They are too consumed in their community, their neighborhood, their streets, and the people in their immediate proximity to have time for much else. *There is enough good work to be done within 50 feet of any given location in which they stand to worry about the next 50 feet beyond that* (emphasis added). They know that others will do that work."[8]

So what lies within your fifty feet?

Case Study: Hot + Water = Servant Evangelism

Some time ago, I (Jeremy) was involved in a servant evangelism project where our congregation handed out four hundred bottles of water in about an hour. It was a great experience, and some folks visited our worship service as a result, but the real goodness was in the details. Here's how it went down.

- *It was hot.* The thermometer was creeping toward one hundred degrees, which in our area (suburban Seattle) is extremely unusual.
- *Traffic was heavy.* The church building used to be in a wooded backwater, but due to lots of residential development, the nearby road was now used by twenty thousand cars a day. You could see the drivers panting.
- *We were sorta stuck.* It was early in my time with a small church whose future was uncertain. We needed some kind of mission work for our own spiritual well-being.
- *I made a decision.* I decided that I was going to pass out water bottles with a little card about our church, pay for this out of my own pocket (no need to get anybody's permission), and that I would stand outside and look like a fool all by myself if need be.
- *I didn't wait, but I did invite.* Fearing that the heat wave might break soon, I sent out an immediate e-mail to

---

[8] Josh is a great photographer, thoughtful blogger, and the son of a preacher man. His blog is http://blog.joshualongbrake.com/

everybody in our little church, essentially saying that I was willing to do all the work myself and spend all the money myself, but if there was anyone crazy enough to join me, they were welcome.

In short, I had an idea, an opportunity, an Internet connection, low expectations, and the willingness to look dumb in public for a short period of time. It was a cross between a humble offering and a desperation move.

Given the context, the results were awesome.

- Within minutes, cases of bottled water, bags of ice, and water coolers started showing up at the church, some given by people of very limited means.
- About eighteen people showed up to pass out water. This was about half of our regular attendance at the time, and none of them had done it before. In those days, it was tough to get volunteers for basic church maintenance, but people seemed to come out of the woodwork for this. Further, the heat was stifling. Despite this, eighteen people signed up to literally go sweat in traffic.
- We talked about this for over a year afterward. I'm not kidding. One good experience was all it took. It was like God unlocked our hearts. And it opened the door for much, much more.

There were a lot of reasons this worked for us, but all of them met at the intersection of dumb luck and God's grace. Looking back, the one thing that stands out to me is that we didn't overthink things. Had circumstances been different, a measured approach may have been more appropriate. Impulsivity or poor planning can dramatically reduce our mission effectiveness. But there comes a point where we have to stop thinking and start doing.

Freeloaders, Heavy Loaders, and Christian Consumers

Servant evangelism is awesome, but we need to be very realistic about our expectations. When it comes to service-oriented outreach efforts, there are three groups of people that we should be aware of.

The first group we call *freeloaders*. Every community has them, people who are happy to be on the receiving end of an uneven relationship. We know hardworking, salt-of-the-earth children's ministry volunteers who decry the passive parents who happily deliver their offspring to church for "free babysitting." We know gluttons who make the rounds to church potlucks and carry-ins to avail themselves of the feeding trough. And we have no problem calling this for what it is: freeloading.

Believe it or not, we're not opposed to serving freeloaders. In fact, we believe that our openhanded service can bless them and teach them (and us) a thing or two about grace and greed. For our part, we cannot let their smallness cause our hearts to shrivel. But when we give to those who have no intention of giving back, we owe it to ourselves to know exactly what we are doing. If we expect our generosity to magically transform takers into givers, we are probably setting ourselves up for disappointment. And our service will not be sustainable if we *only* reach out to those who have no desire to reach back.

The second group we call *heavy loaders*. We're also convinced that every community, regardless of appearances, has people who are barely holding on. We've seen this in single parents, the working poor, those with debilitating medical issues, even in two-parent households where Mom and Dad are about to lose their jobs or their house and are both working double shifts to make ends meet. It can include people who've made bad choices, people who've received bad chances, or some combination of both. It even includes mature believers who simply get overwhelmed with

151

a series of major life transitions and need to subsist in a season of receiving.

We bring this up because servants need to make a distinction between freeloaders and heavy loaders and because from the outside it can be hard to tell the difference between the two. But there is a great difference. Whereas freeloaders could give back and don't want to, heavy loaders may want to give back and simply can't. They are functioning at, or often beyond, their capacity. We know one single mother who arranged her meager work schedule around the free children's programming of her neighborhood church. She never made it to a worship service and probably never will. In her case, the children's programming of this congregation was less like a church growth strategy and more like a way to help this family scrape by.

Obviously, we're not opposed to serving heavy loaders. Bless them. Show them mercy. Your church's ministries can be a lifeline to them. And there have been seasons of our own life where *we* have been them. But those of us on the giving end need to be keenly aware of our own expectations and our own capacity. Our generosity may give others some much-needed breathing room, but in many cases, it will not be enough to provide a wholesale social rescue. And at the risk of sounding redundant, serving heavy loaders is a beautiful and worthwhile mission that will not always be an effective church growth strategy. Sadly, sometimes even the best compassion ministries have a way of becoming unsustainable, especially if we *only* reach out to those who do not have the ability to reach back.

The third group is one we call *Christian consumers.* Perhaps this is a special type of freeloader, but we need to make the distinction. It looks like this. One suburban community has a large number of church-active Christians. This same community has a large number of churches that do summer Vacation Bible School for kids. But every summer, there are church-active, Christian parents who routinely sign their children up for every free VBS in town. When they do this without lifting a finger to help out in the effort, it equals free summer camp for the kiddos. In another example, we know of some teens that attend the youth activities of three or more youth groups but give back to zero groups. One friend, a youth pastor, was startled to get a phone call from a teen who offered the following criticism. "Why don't we go on fun ski trips like my other two youth groups?" This youth pastor refers to these teens as "youth groupies," and such an entitlement mentality is profoundly disheartening.

To clarify: As much as this may cause some of us to cringe, it's really not all bad. A parent could do worse than sign up his or her children for a summer's worth of free Bible school. On the other hand, this very real dynamic makes life complicated for the churches that host, lead, and foot the bill for these ministries. This is especially true when the congregations who provide them are counting on their outreach potential. We think we are sowing seeds when sometimes we are servicing the growing appetite for programs in an already existing religious market.

So what do we do with freeloaders, heavy loaders, and Christian consumers? Serve anyway. Give and expect nothing back. Pray for generosity, a fruit of the Holy Spirit. But we'll also say this: make sure you are serving more than just freeloaders, heavy loaders, and Christian consumers. It may be that the majority of people you touch fall into these seemingly unresponsive categories. But if we reach out broadly and consistently, do good follow-up with people who seem interested, and serve with realistic expectations, our churches will have a reasonable chance with a spiritually responsive minority. Not only that, if we do the right thing and publicize it well, people in our community may look at our church and say, "I want to be part of a group of people who do *that*." In this case, the people you attract and the people you serve may be two completely different groups.

Follow Up!

We know great churches that host fun events, initiate superb servant evangelism projects, and put on top-notch activities for kids. Then when the activity is over, they sit back and wait for the unchurched, unbelieving masses to line up for Sunday worship. It rarely happens.

There have never been so many resources, choices, options, and ideas for creative community outreach. It's not hard to find millions of pencils, pens, teddy bears, and toothbrushes stamped with the phrase "Jesus Loves You," and we can hand them out by the trailer load if we want to. But it probably won't amount to anything if we don't follow up.

Follow up. Then follow up on the follow-up. Then follow up again. The end of the event is the beginning of the real work. This is what it takes to turn contacts into friends.

Here are a few tips:

- *Don't* make excuses. Period. *Do* find solutions. You can do this.
- *Don't* neglect to collect names and contact information. Almost all follow-up depends on this crucial step.
- *Don't* count on the initiative of the signer-uppers. If you stick a pen and an attendance pad in someone's face, they probably won't fill it out. Or they won't fill it out completely. Or they won't fill it out legibly, even if it screams in all caps PLEASE FILL OUT THIS FORM COMPLETELY AND LEGIBLY across the top of the page. Maybe people are more compliant and do a better job of following directions where you live, but in our experience this rarely works.
- *Do* take the initiative to creatively collect relevant contact information and recruit a lovely human being who will be responsible for getting the data. Recruit a

Boy Scout or Girl Scout in uniform. Dress up a little girl in a tutu and a tiara and equip her with a pink ink pen and a sparkly sign-in pad. Find a kind, nonthreatening, sincere, sweet-faced extroverted adult who is good with eye contact. Then turn them loose! Have them say, "We are really glad you are here. And we want to keep you in the loop. Can we send you an invitation to things like this in the future?" Have your volunteers wait patiently and make small talk while the sheet is filled out. Have them confirm spelling. Or have the sweet-faced extrovert fill the sheet out for them. Have the attendee use an iPad rather than pencil and paper, eliminating the need for legible handwriting. Use a raffle or drawing or give away an iPad if you need to, but get that contact information and make a good impression while doing so!

- *Do not* send a form letter. Please. Send something funny, something creative, something unusual. I know it seems efficient ("My secretary assembled four hundred follow-up letters in two hours!"), but if nobody reads your missive, it doesn't matter how efficient you were ("My secretary wasted two hours assembling milquetoast junk mail that was immediately pitched!"). And pastors, watch your language. We're all tempted to try to sound profound and theological, but if our verbiage smacks of seminarian Shakespeare, we might as well be speaking in tongues. Heck, speaking in tongues would probably be more memorable!

- *Do* the inefficient, small-scale, one-to-one follow-up. Did you strike up a conversation with an attendee at your event whose mother was going in to surgery next week? Note the date and send a card. Did you meet with someone who might be interested in partnering with your church in some way? Even if it's a long shot, ask them to coffee

155

next week just to talk about possibilities. Did you briefly connect with a person who happened to tell you their name? Friend them on Facebook. Is someone willing to pose for a picture? Take their photo on your smartphone, upload it to your church's social media site, and tag them immediately. Did you run into an angry young man or woman who was hesitant to socialize? Give that angst a good outlet! Send them a text, give them a call, or drop off a brochure and ask them to consider joining your church on your next service or justice project. I know you can't do all of this, so recruit one or two or twenty people from your church to show up and mingle and then do follow-up afterward.

Service Is Not Enough

Here's the deal. Churches used to think that building a neat-o facility was the key to building good worship attendance. Although it's not in the Bible, the phrase "If we build it, they will come" was treated as Scripture. Of course, it's not that simple, and many of us have learned that lesson the hard way. But here is another truism we need to discard: "If we serve them, they will come." Serving people is no guarantee that they will show up on Sundays at 10:00 a.m. to listen to our venerated pipe organ or cool guitars.

Here's something that is in Scripture: "I do not call you servants any longer ... but I have called you friends" (John 15:15). Consider the fact that serving someone else can be a way of keeping them at a distance. We can hide behind our acts of service. But we can also begin a friendship with someone by serving them.

We need to see our church's service efforts for what they are—a priceless opportunity to love others in a practical way while *building our church's relational network.* Servant evangelism is not just religious advertising. It is an opportunity to build bridges, develop community, and establish relationships with those we are serving. It's not about getting the job done. It's about building the relationship. Because the relationship *is* the job.

Begin as servants, but become friends.

About E³ Ministry Group

As a favor to a friend, I once worked the book table at a Christian conference. The table was brimming with curriculums, programs, and publications for sale. One attendee approached me, looked at all the resources, and declared, "I never know if they are equipping us or marketing us."

This attendee put his finger on the problem of most church "experts" - **one size fits none.**

Your church is different. It's a unique community and culture. And it's supposed to be. Your church doesn't need a random expert pushing a prefabricated program. You need an approachable practitioner who **engages** with you by asking:

> What is life like in *your* neighborhood?
> What thrives in *your* context?
> **What is Christ calling *you* to do?**

This book is the first resource produced by E³ Ministry Group. We're a team of experienced, creative, and innovative coaches and consultants with a passion for bringing **renewal, vitality, and revitalization** to God's people and our congregations. We've worked with churches both large (6000 people) and small (15 people) to offer collaborative guidance, customized solutions, and a "hands-on" partnership.

Some of our specialties include:
- Faith Sharing
- Leadership Development
- Christian Hospitality
- Children & Youth Ministry
- Stewardship
- Congregational Life & Vibrancy
- Discipleship Ministries
- Building and Facilities Assessment

For more on relevant resources, speaking engagements, trainings, coaching, and consulting, please contact us!

E³ Ministry Group
Info@E3MinistryGroup.com
1-855-639-6990
456 Myers Avenue
Harrisonburg, VA 22801